# 3 Word Rebellion

## CREATE A ONE-OF-A-KIND MESSAGE THAT GROWS YOUR BUSINESS INTO A MOVEMENT

*Michelle A. Mazur, Ph.D.*

3 Word Rebellion: Create a Message Bigger than You and Your Business
By Michelle A. Mazur

Designed by Natalie McGuire

For information on getting permission for reprints and excerpts, contact: hello@drmichellemazur.com

ISBN: 9798985220803

Published by Communication Rebel Press, Seattle, WA.
Communication Rebel is a registered trademark of Relationally Speaking, LLC

# In memory of my darling, obsessive Lola Cat.

*I miss your purr and watching you eat.*

*To my husband, Glenn.*

*You make my life possible.*

*I love you.*

*(And thanks for understanding why Lola got top billing.)*

# TABLE OF CONTENTS

# A Permission from the Book

## THE ACT OF PURCHASING THIS BOOK TELLS ME AND THIS BOOK SOMETHING VERY IMPORTANT ABOUT YOU.

## IT TELLS US SOMETHING THAT MAYBE HARD FOR YOU TO ACCEPT OR EVEN BEGIN TO BELIEVE.

So, what do we know about you?

Here it goes. We believe that the message you have rolling around in your head is massively important. It's powerful. It deserves an audience, and it needs you to champion it. I believe that you are a thought leader. This book knows you are too. In my heart, I know you have a thought or two in your big brain right now that could change people's lives, your industry, or even the world.

This Book and I wanted you to know that straight away. It's okay if you don't see yourself as a "thought leader" right now. By doing the exercises in this book, the perception of how you see yourself will begin to shift. In the meantime, you're welcome to borrow my belief in your leadership!

Speaking of doing the exercises, the book you're holding in your hands is designed for you to write in. Highlight passages. Doodle in the margins. Complete the exercises. Use it as your messaging journal.

On these pages, pour out your creative mess!

I want you to love and use this book like you would love

and use your favorite journal. This Book wants to go to coffee shops with you. This Book wants your kids to scribble on its cover. This Book wants a glass of wine spilled on it (this Book loves a good Pinot Noir #justsayin).

This book is *beautiful*. (If I dare say so myself.) I intentionally designed it so that you would want to buy the hard copy. In fact, I decided not to even offer a Kindle version of this book because This Book and I want you use it. We are dedicated to you finding your 3 Word Rebellion.

I wanted you to hold this book in your hand. Luxuriate in its heft. Feel the weight of the paper as you turn each page.

I have purchased a ton of well-designed, gorgeous books, and I know how I am when I get a beautiful book. I want to keep those books in pristine condition even though the authors ask me to do the exercises and urge me to scribble in it.

Despite their persuasive attempts, you know what I didn't do? *Write in those books.* I didn't complete the exercises. I didn't want to ruin the aesthetic. I didn't do what the books' authors intended me to do: use the damn book!

When I didn't use those books, I didn't get the transformation that the authors promised. The same will happen here unless you *use the book.* **Because the truth is, the only way to find your 3 Word Rebellion is to write.** Getting your ideas out of your head and on paper makes them concrete. You'll be able to see patterns, connections, and what ideas need to fall away.

THIS BOOK (AND I)
GIVE YOU PERMISSION TO SCRIBBLE
ALL OVER IT.

# We give you permission to use the damn book!

Go wild. What's most important to me and the book is that you find your 3 Word Rebellion. That you launch that rebellion into the world. That you build a message that is bigger than you and your business.

And you can't do that if you treat this book like a work of art. Get messy with it. This Book and I thank you.


Yours in Rebellion,

*Michelle (and this Book)*

# INTRODUCTION:

# Make Communication Matter Again

**A**t age six, I jumped off the little yellow school bus and ran up to my big yellow house, so excited that I nearly peed my pants.

I figured out my life's plan. I knew exactly what I wanted to do and exactly how I wanted to change the world. I couldn't wait to tell the one person who mattered most to me.

"Mom, Mom, I know what I want to be when I grow up!"

She stopped what she was doing and beamed at me with delight, "Great, honey, what's that?"

I stammered with the excitement of it all, "Mom, I want to be a...a...a...POLITICIAN."

She looked a bit perplexed by my epiphany. "Oh, you want to be president?"

"No, Mom, not president...a politician."

"Why's that?"

"Because politicians help people."

I don't know who put that idea into my head. All I know is that I was a weird kid with huge aspirations (and I would wager since you're reading a book about creating a message that is bigger than your business that you also have a big audacious vision).

Not only did I want to be a politician, but at this young age I already knew where I stood on policies. The first presidential election I can remember was Carter vs. Reagan in 1980. I wanted President Carter to stay in office because I thought he was a good man who was trying to help. I was ticked off that I couldn't vote in this election, so I lobbied my parents to vote for Jimmy Carter. I am sure that my mom did, but I am *pretty* sure my dad went for Reagan.

As did the rest of the country in a landslide.

Even at my school's mock election, I was one of two people in my entire school who voted for Carter. The funny thing was that everyone in my school *knew* that one of those votes was mine.

How did that happen? How does someone so young have political aspirations?

It's my Mom's fault!

My mom raised me on the speeches of Martin Luther King Jr. She told me stories about John F. Kennedy and his famous speech where he said, "Ask not what your country can do for you. Ask what you can do for your country." My mom loved Bobby Kennedy and all the work he was doing for the civil rights movement.

What I remember most was how these men made her feel. They gave her hope for the country. I also remember her tears and anger. How she cried all night the day President Kennedy was assassinated in Dallas. The anger and sadness over the murder of Dr. King. The utter despair when Bobby was mortally wounded in the Ambassador Hotel in Los Angeles.

She felt hope die when each of these men was murdered. Not me. In my optimistic brain, I saw these men dying for a cause. Sacrificing to help people. They died trying to make the country and even the world better. Even as a young child, I felt called to change the world too. Their lives gave me hope.

As I grew, I was able to hear their words for myself.

> THE SPEECHES OF THESE GREAT
> MEN GAVE ME THE IMPRESSION
> THAT COMMUNICATION CHANGES
> THE WORLD.
>
> AND IT DOES. FOR BETTER OR FOR
> WORSE, DAY AFTER DAY.

Although my political aspirations were dashed in a crushing loss in the race for student council in the third grade, I still believe that communication changes the world.

I started Communication Rebel with that mission in mind. I work with coaches, consultants, serviced-based business owners, speakers and entrepreneurs to create that message that is bigger than them and their business. My clients want to go from running an expert business to being a thought leader. To make that leap, they need a message that takes on a life of its own and spreads in ways the messenger could hardly imagine.

Although I love my change-making clients, what I saw in the speaking industry pissed me off. What I saw in the online business world made me sick to my stomach. I saw communication being weaponized. I saw powerful persuasion tactics being employed not to benefit people, but to make the business owner and the speaker more money.

I witnessed people (myself included) paying $2,000 or even $3,000 for a do-it-yourself course they really didn't need, all because of the fear of missing out. They believed this course would be a miracle cure that would solve all of their ails (it wouldn't).

Speakers and business owners became more obsessed with scaling their business to seven or even eight figures in 30 seconds or less and getting themselves out of their business so they could make money in their sleep.

The industry lost its moral compass (if it ever had one to begin with) because of Bro Marketing.

Bro Marketing uses psychological triggers (e.g., scarcity, authority, social proof, etc.) to shut down critical thinking skills and eliminate consent to manipulate people into buying. Instead of business owners making **the best purchasing decision for themselves**, they are coerced into buying because of fear of missing out (FOMO), manufactured authority, Neuro-Linguistic Programming (NLP) hacks, plain old fear, and so much more.

Bro marketing is the air we breathe and the water we swim in for the online world. It's taught as the ONLY way to market and sell, but, my rebel friend, there is another way.

## BRO MARKETING WEAPONIZES COMMUNICATION.

Side note: Women can 100% be bro marketers. Just because you have a vagina doesn't mean you're immune. I call it Bro Marketing as a wink and a nod to the patriarchy; the top-down authoritarian way to communicate that says, *"I know better than you about what you need. What you need is to buy my thing and it will take away all of your problems."*

HERE'S THE REBEL TRUTH:

# THESE BUSINESS OWNERS & SPEAKERS, USING BRO MARKETER TACTICS, WERE NOT USING COMMUNICATION TO CHANGE THE WORLD.

THEY WERE USING IT TO LINE THEIR POCKETS AND SECURE BRAGGING RIGHTS FOR A SIX-FIGURE LAUNCH SO THEY COULD THEN TEACH OTHERS HOW TO DO THE SAME.

## THE ONLINE BUSINESS WORLD SPOTLIGHTS BRO MARKETING AS THE FASTEST AND ONLY PATH TO CASH.

Now, I don't have anything against making money. *I love money.* I love it because it allows me to do good in the world, to travel, and to live a nice life with my husband and three cats. I strongly believe we need money as a resource to do our work in the world. However, the industry became about profit over impact (that's *not* okay). These speakers and business owners abdicated their leadership role in their industry.

When an industry that is supposed to produce change and results for its clients, audiences, businesses, and the world focuses on money over impact, that's when communication stops mattering. It's when communication *stops* changing the world.

## IT'S TIME TO MAKE COMMUNICATION MATTER AGAIN.

It's time to elevate speakers, business owners, and entrepreneurs to rebel leaders so that they use their power of influence for the greater good.

When you and I start communicating to change people, our industry, and even the world, we leave a lasting legacy. We profit *because* of our impact, not in spite of it.

I'll be honest, I fell for all of that "six figures in six seconds" hype too. I was afraid of missing out on the magical solution that would change my business if I didn't press the *Buy Now* button before the clock ran out. Deep down all of that hype felt soulless to me, but I didn't follow my intuition. I followed what I thought would work. Until I decided to stop and make communication matter again. I'll tell you all about that journey in Chapter One, where I explain the concept of the 3 Word Rebellion.

This book is meant to give you the tools to rise up as the rebel leader you are and communicate the change you want to see in the world. And not only communicate that change, but build a movement around it.

There has never been a time when we are more in need of business owners and speakers who are focused on making a difference, who want to lead and challenge the status quo and change things for the better.

Communication needs to matter again. This book outlines another way for you to serve and sell more without compromising your values. It's about creating a marketing message that does good in the world.

If you want to change the world, you must craft a message that matters to other people. You must have a message that calls people into your movement.

You must have a message that is bigger than you and your business.

You must do more than spread ideas. Those ideas are adding to the noise. We've had enough ideas spreading like a virus on the Internet for years now. Those ideas are not making a lick of difference because people don't *do* anything with those ideas.

> ## YOUR AUDIENCE MUST *ACT* ON YOUR MESSAGE FOR THINGS TO CHANGE.

In order to incite action, your message must resonate. Your people must grok it quickly and experience the results that it brings. This is why the 3 Word Rebellion works. It's a short, memorable message that recruits people into your rebellion. In this book I'll walk you through the entire process of how to create your own 3 Word Rebellion.

In Chapter One, I'm going to explain the origin of the 3 Word Rebellion and how by looking at theories from social movements and analyzing the careers of successful speakers and business owners I discovered a pattern and framework for crafting your 3 Word Rebellion.

In Chapter Two, I'm elevating you from business owner to the Rebel Leader of your movement who uses your influence and voice for the greater good.

In Chapter Three, I'll discuss why you should be starting a movement around your message and your business. I realize that asking you to create a message that is bigger than you and your business is a huge ask. I want to show you why this works (and help you discover your own motivation to do it).

In Chapter Four, I walk you through the framework and give you a bit of homework to do. Don't worry, it's fun and can involve wine or craft beer (I'm more of a craft beer girl myself). Answering the powerful questions posed in this chapter gives you the raw material to craft your 3 Word Rebellion.

Chapter Five shows you how to analyze that raw material to find the right words that move people into action. It will also illuminate what holds people back from writing their 3 Word Rebellion and show you how to strengthen yours so that it sticks in your audience's mind and spreads your message.

Chapter Six is meant to give you inspiration to take action on writing your 3 Word Rebellion. I analyze five 3 Word Rebellions and explain why they work and what you can learn from each of them.

In Chapter Seven, you'll put your 3 Word Rebellion to the ultimate test. In case you're wondering if your 3 Word Rebellion is any "good," this chapter helps you answer the question through a very simple framework based on neuroscience.

In Chapter Eight, you'll discover all the supporting messages you need to persuade people to hire you and join your movement.

In the final chapter, I talk about what comes next after you discover your 3 Word Rebellion: the inciting incident that launches your 3 Word Rebellion into the world.

This book is meant to be short and interactive so that you can find your 3 Word Rebellion and launch it into the world as soon as possible. Do the work, complete the writing exercises, and you'll find your 3 Word Rebellion.

Here's a secret, **I believe your 3 Word Rebellion already exists**. You simply must excavate it from all of the thoughts and ideas that you have. You must see its value and how it helps people. It's waiting for you, and we will start finding it in Chapter One!

# CHAPTER ONE:

# Introducing the 3 Word Rebellion

**B**efore I tell you how the 3 Word Rebellion rose like a phoenix out of the ashes of my business, I want to tell you what it is and what it can do for you, your business, and even the world.

## WHAT IS THE 3 WORD REBELLION?

At its core, the 3 Word Rebellion encapsulates the change you want to create in the world with your message. The 3 Word Rebellion gathers your audience, helps them take action, and then encourages them to share your message with others. It also leads your right people to work with you to experience that change in their lives. It's simple and powerfully persuasive.

A 3 Word Rebellion is a message that demands attention. It performs three jobs in your business.

The first job a 3 Word Rebellion does is call your "right" audience in. You need other people to follow your lead. You need other people who value you what you value. You need other people to be a part of the change you're creating. You need other people to be your clients! As Derek Sivers says in his brilliant three-minute TED talk "How to Start a Movement," "The first follower transforms the lone nut into a leader." The 3 Word Rebellion recruits your first follower and many more people into your movement.

The second job that a 3 Word Rebellion does is incite your audience to take action because it's focused on a result and the change that you see for them. When a person hears your 3 Word

Rebellion, it tells people the next action to take.

The final job the 3 Word Rebellion does is allow these followers to spread your message for you. They say, "Hell yes!" They get a result that changes them through your work and then start to talk to other people about that change.

What happens when people start spreading your message? More people find out about it. They google it and take action. They start talking about your message. It begins to snowball. You and your message are gaining momentum. You're getting more clients hungry to work with you. You're impacting more people. You're changing your industry. And yes, you're even making the world a better place in your own unique way. **The 3 Word Rebellion creates a ripple effect of change.**

What does this momentum do for you? It gives you name recognition and positions you as the thought leader of the movement that you are creating (more on leadership in the next chapter).

Having a 3 Word Rebellion provides you with more opportunity. More opportunity to work with clients you love. Opportunity to speak on stages. Opportunity to impact more people.

Now, your business is memorable. The change you want to create and the results your work promises are clear. Why people should care is clear. When your message gels like that, everything becomes easier. More media appearances, podcast interviews, and speaking opportunities come your way. Clients want to work with you. Book deals happen. People start changing the world with you so you don't have to go it alone. Your 3 Word Rebellion will change your business.

Ultimately, the 3 Word Rebellion is the hook that demands attention. These three words demand that people slow their scroll and read more about it. It instantly gets people to sit up and pay attention to your message. It's the change you want to create. It's the ultimate pitch. It's the story you're telling. It's the topic you want to be known for. It's the action the audience should take. It's everything your business needs wrapped up in three words.

## THE ORIGIN OF THE 3 WORD REBELLION

I discovered the power of the 3 Word Rebellion when I hit the "I can't keep doing this" point in my business. The 3 Word Rebellion came out of utter frustration. After six years of blogging and podcasting about speaking, I had a moment of "what the hell am I going to talk about next year?"

I was done. I was done talking about how to get speaking gigs, how to make money speaking, and how to market your business and get clients with speaking without selling from the stage.

**I was over all of it.** It wasn't that this information wasn't useful. It was. I knew these were the questions that my audience wanted answered, but it was unfulfilling for me. Honestly, my audience was one Google search away from finding this information, so it didn't have to be me who published it.

I took some time off and thought about what I was doing with this business and what I wanted to create. I also started daydreaming about my imaginary boyfriend, Simon Sinek, who reminded me to start with why.

As I explained in the Introduction, my why has always been that communication changes the world.

In the past few years of my business, I grew apart from that why. In fact, it felt like I had abandoned my why on the side of the road somewhere in rural Missouri.

HERE'S THE REBEL TRUTH:

# I BELIEVED THE ONLY WAY YOU CAN HAVE A SIX-, SEVEN-, OR GAZILLION-FIGURE BUSINESS WAS TO GIVE PEOPLE WHAT THEY WANT.

AND I GOT CAUGHT UP IN THE IDEA THAT THE ONLY THING PEOPLE WILL PAY FOR IS WHAT THEY CAN MAKE MONEY WITH.

I bought into the Bro Marketing hype (even I, who knows better with my fancy Ph.D. in Communication, got swallowed whole by this marketing).

While I'm fiercely committed to speakers getting *paid* for their work on stage, I realized the best way to make that happen is to focus on *impact* and the profit will come. I had been too focused on helping people make money and was ignoring my belief in the importance of impact.

Money is not the only result we give to clients. You and I change our clients in tangible and intangible ways. I forgot that truth.

Now, my clients were always focused on the change and the results they wanted to give their audience, so I was talking to the right people. But I was totally out of alignment with my core belief, and my burnout showed that!

So I sat with it. It was one of those riddles that I knew I couldn't figure out by creating a 90-day content plan. It was something that could only be solved by sitting with it, asking friends, family, and the universe about it, and knowing the answer would come.

The answer came from the least likely place: Facebook.

## MEL ROBBINS SAVES THE DAY AND MY BUSINESS

As I was scrolling mindlessly through my Facebook feed one day, I saw a video called "Why Motivation Is Garbage."

Oh...that grabbed my attention. I'm always going on about how motivating an audience never works and motivation on its own is a waste of persuasion. I watched this video and I was mesmerized.

I googled the speaker, Mel Robbins, and found her book *The 5 Second Rule.* Curious as to what this "rule" was, I googled more and found her TEDx talk about it.

I loved her. I loved the idea of the 5 Second Rule. I loved how it was inspiring people to take action.

And then I got pissed off!

I earned a doctorate in communication. I spent years in academia building complex models and theories. **And you mean to tell me that this Mel Robbins person built her *entire* platform around telling people to count backwards from five and take an action?**

5-4-3-2-1 ACT. That's the 5 Second Rule.

You're kidding, right? People pay for that?

The answer is *yes.* Yes, they do pay for that—Mel Robbins was the most-booked female speaker in 2017.

Then it hit me why.

Simplicity. The 5 Second Rule is so simple to use. The people who watch Mel speak get instant results from it. Organizations see an immediate change in the people who work for them when those employees use it. It's so bloody useful and it helps people become who they want to be.

Mel Robbins was making communication matter again every time she spoke (or tweeted or Instagrammed or Facebooked).

The 5 Second Rule is brilliant and it is everything that I tell my speakers to do: give your audience *one* result (not three, not five, just one) and they will be dedicated to you because you changed them. You made a *meaningful difference* in their lives.

Those people that Mel impacted started to talk about the 5 Second Rule. They shared it on social media. They became fans and followers for life. She was changing the world. She had created a movement with her message.

There it was—she created a *movement*.

That's how speakers, entrepreneurs, business owners, and healers change the world with communication. They create a movement. They have a message that others rally around, identify with, and are impacted by. The people who are changed want to share that transformation with others. The message takes on a life of its own and becomes the movement.

All of a sudden, I needed to know more about social movements

## WHAT SOCIAL MOVEMENTS AND MEL ROBBINS HAVE IN COMMON

I'm a researcher at heart, so I did what I do best. I took one class about social movements in graduate school, so I didn't feel surefooted around the theories. I stumbled upon and devoured Jonathan Fields' *The Art of Revolution*. I then raided the references throughout that book for more reading material (that's an advanced grad school hack...find one article and then read all the other material cited in it).

While I loved what Fields created in his manifesto, I felt it was too much. It was too complex and overwhelming for anyone to tackle. He'd presented 18 steps to start a revolution (so this was the antithesis of the uber-simple 5 Second Rule). I wanted to create something simple that speakers, business owners, entrepreneurs, nonprofits, and anyone who wants to make a change in the world could grok and immediately use.

I wanted to create the 5 Second Rule for movement making.

Around the same time, I was watching a lot of news (which isn't the best for my mental health and yet I felt the need to stay informed). I could feel the winds of change sweeping over America. I read stories about movements that were rising up in America:

* Black Lives Matter
* Make America Great Again
* #TimesUp
* #MeToo
* March for Our Lives

My mind is always making connections and spotting patterns. I began to think of the speakers I greatly admired and loved to watch:

* Simon Sinek (Start with Why)
* Sally Hogshead (How to Fascinate)
* Mel Robbins (5 Second Rule)

I realized that the rallying cries of movements and successful speakers' messages had an obvious similarity: a short and memorable phrase or name was associated with each. I started to wonder if I could use the framework of movement making to help my clients develop their core message.

I did, and it worked. It worked exceedingly well. People who had been struggling to define their message for *years* were now doing so in 30 minutes or less.

I was on to something that could not only help speakers but could help anyone who wants to make a difference in the world.

Eureka! I had the framework for the 3 Word Rebellion. Now that leads to the question that everyone is asking me these days...

# WHAT'S MY 3 WORD REBELLION?

Surprise, surprise, it's 3 Word Rebellion (I'm meta like that!).

Why *3*? People remember best what they hear in threes.

Why *words*? Words move your people to act, call them into your movement and business, and let them spread your message.

Why *rebellion*? Communication changes the world. To shake up your audience, your industry, and the world, you must rebel against the status quo.

To be clear, I was a rebel long before I figured out my 3 Word Rebellion. This framework is a synthesis of all the work I've been doing my entire life. My 3 Word Rebellion has been waiting for me to discover it all of these years. Your 3 Word Rebellion is waiting for you too!

Finding my own 3 Word Rebellion and developing this framework changed everything in my business. I saw people on social media talking about their 3 Word Rebellion. I had an easy time pitching myself for podcast interviews because my message was so unique. Clients started to come to me specifically for this work.

It started snowballing. Most importantly, my work mattered to me again. I saw that communication did in fact change the world and that people were excited to step up to leadership.

WHEN YOU IDENTIFY AND SHARE
YOUR 3 WORD REBELLION, YOU'RE
AN UNSTOPPABLE FORCE FOR
GOOD.

You're elevated to a leader with powerful influence. You're on the road to becoming a thought leader.

While all that may sound enticing, it's probably sinking in that what I am asking you to do is *big*. So let's dig into that— because you need to be prepared to lead before you can create the message that starts a movement.

# CHAPTER TWO:

# Embodying the Rebel Leader

**T**he 3 Word Rebellion calls you to build something much bigger than a business or a nonprofit; it calls you to build something with *impact*. Something that has the potential to change lives or even society.

The 3 Word Rebellion calls you to start a movement, and it calls you to step into leadership. Why? Because every movement needs a leader, or the movement fizzles. Remember the Occupy Wall Street movement? They were rebelling against the 1% controlling most of the wealth. But the movement didn't have a leader. In fact that movement openly scorned the idea of having a leader. Because there was no one to lead, they could not articulate the change they wanted to create or how they would go about it. Their battle cry was Wall Street Sucks, but there was no leader to drive the movement forward, so it petered out.

I'm calling you to step into something huge, something that you are at the epicenter of. You're the catalyst, the change maker, the business owner and speaker making it happen.

In essence, I'm asking you to lead. To embody the rebel leader and build momentum for your message.

While that might be intriguing to you, it also might be freaking you out.

I want to address this early. I know for myself that when I started talking about the impact of a strong message and the opportunity to build a movement, I became freakishly excited about the possibilities of what I was creating—and also completely terrified.

Who am I to lead this 3 Word Rebellion movement? I'm not

really a leader, I thought. Do I have what it takes to pull this off?

If you're feeling like I did, then it's time we meet that resistance head on.

## MINDSET SHIFT AHEAD:
## YOU ARE A LEADER!

To thwart resistance, the first thing you must embrace is a shift in your identity.

THE REBEL TRUTH:

# IF YOU ARE A BUSINESS OWNER, SPEAKER, ENTREPRENEUR, OR HEAD OF A NONPROFIT, GUESS WHAT? YOU'RE ALREADY A LEADER.

SURPRISE!

If you don't yet see yourself as a leader, you're not alone. My clients and I often come up against the issue that many people in our audiences don't identify as leaders. This means that they don't think a leadership message applies to them.

I too had a problem identifying as a leader. I saw myself as a humble servant helping my clients make more money with speaking by creating an epic audience experience. I didn't think I was a leader, just a passionate business owner.

I thought that leaders were CEOs like Jeff Bezos or Bill Gates, or people facilitating huge cultural discussions like Brené Brown, or political figures like Presidents Barack Obama, Ronald Reagan, or John F. Kennedy.

I'm still doing the work of owning the power and responsibility of being a leader, but it became much easier when I realized this truth: to be a leader, you must step into the role.

IF YOU WANT A TAILORED
ACTION PLAN TO GET OUT OF
YOUR OWN WAY AND STEP INTO
YOUR LEADERSHIP,
GO TAKE THE QUIZ, "WHAT'S YOUR
REBEL ROADMAP TO EXPONENTIAL
IMPACT + INFLUENCE?"

IT WILL GIVE YOU A HUGE MINDSET
SHIFT TO FULLY EMBODY YOUR ROLE.
**WWW.THEREBELQUIZ.COM.**

REBEL TRUTH:

# YOU CAN'T TRANSFORM EVEN ONE PERSON IF YOU'RE NOT READY TO LEAD!

You and I are in this game because we want to make a difference, change people, and transform our industries. That is what drives you and me: we are rebel leaders and we are rising up to create change.

The moment you speak in front of a group or on Facebook Live, you're a speaker, and the moment you are a speaker in front of a group, you are a leader, because you are trying to influence the actions the audience will take after hearing your message (unless you are just an entertainer, but even stand up comedians are often trying to create some change with their comedy).

In order to fully realize your goals and dreams, you need to accept and start growing into this identity. It's your job to lead! Once you accept that, you're a step closer to making a bigger impact with your work.

As I've been exploring what it means to embody the role of rebel leader, I have found that leaders of movements have three characteristics. First, a leader owns her power and wields that power with great care. Second, she is a steward of the change that she wants to bring forth into the world. Finally, she is wildly devoted and committed to her following.

## EMBRACE YOUR POWER
## WHILE USING IT RESPONSIBLY

It's important to recognize that the 3 Word Rebellion is powerful. It's powerful for creating change. It's powerful for spreading your message. It's powerful for recruiting people into your movement. In short, **your 3 Word Rebellion allows you to wield power and influence.**

AND AS UNCLE BEN IN *SPIDERMAN* SAID, "WITH GREAT POWER COMES GREAT RESPONSIBILITY."

The 3 Word Rebellion can be used for good or evil. It could be used for a good cause like stopping shootings in schools or ending sexual harassment. It can also be used for evil like manipulating people to buy products they don't really need or even starting your own "end of the world" cult.

I hate to think of this concept being used for evil, and I'd be remiss and a bad former academic if I didn't dive into the ethics of using your 3 Word Rebellion.

**A rebel leader is an ethical leader.** This means the movement you're creating makes the world better. It means that you've spent time thinking through the implications of the change you are creating in the world. How is this change going to impact people directly? How is it going to change your industry and society? Could there be any unintended consequences that would harm people further?

*Don't worry if you don't know all of the answers to these questions now.* You can think all of this through later. First, you need to zero in on the change you want to create. Then, at the end of Chapter Four, I'll be walking you through an exercise to help you consider the ethical ramifications of your rebellion.

It's paramount that you make decisions based on what's best for your audience and the people who follow you and not merely what is best for your own personal interests. It boils down to trust and goodwill. People will follow you when they know that you have their best interests in mind. Those people will proudly share about your message, your movement, and your business because you care and put them first.

Do what is best for your people, and use the 3 Word Rebellion for the greater good of all of us!

I, _____,

(STATE YOUR NAME)

## SOLEMNLY SWEAR THAT

# I WILL ONLY USE THE 3 WORD REBELLION FOR GOOD.

·

## BE COMMITTED TO CHANGE
## AND TRANSFORMATION

Now that we've chatted about the first trait of a rebel leader and I've gotten your commitment to do good with your 3 Word Rebellion, let's dive into the second trait that helps you embody your role.

> REBEL LEADERS ARE THE AMBASSADORS OF THE CHANGE THEY WANT TO CREATE.

They are not only the ambassador, they are committed to seeing that change happen for their audience and industry.

A rebel leader follows her audience as much as they follow her. She wants to see that they get results from the work that they are doing in the world. Because if change is not happening, it is up to that leader to take a different course.

Beto O'Rourke, who ran for Senate against Ted Cruz in Texas in 2018, is a perfect example of a leader who is committed to the change he wants to create for the people in his state. O'Rourke's 3 Word Rebellion is "No PACs. Just people."

He is fiercely committed to getting corporate money out of politics, so he didn't take a dime from PACs or special interest groups. He wanted to represent the people of Texas, *not* corporations. His promise to Texans was simple: give everyone a chance to succeed.

O'Rourke's commitment to this vision means he went to every county in Texas (even those that have not voted for a Democrat in decades) to meet the people, hear their thoughts, and find out their challenges. He invited people who disagree with him to come to his events and speak to him because he wanted to know their concerns. That's commitment.

According to CNN, O'Rourke out-fundraised Cruz, with 10 million dollars to Cruz's four million dollars. Over two hundred thousand individuals donated to O'Rourke's campaign compared to the roughly 1,200 individuals who donated to Cruz.

Although O'Rourke ultimately lost to Cruz, he gained a committed following. O'Rourke leads his people and continues to be a beacon of change in Texas.

As a leader, you can do this too. Soon, oh so soon, you'll be figuring out what change you want to see in the world (I'll walk you through it). When your focus is on the delivery of your promise, your message becomes bigger than your speech, bigger than just another Facebook Live, another business deal, or another fundraising event.

It starts becoming a movement.

Take a moment now (or come back to this question after you've done the 3 Word Rebellion exercises) to brainstorm.

# WHAT CAN YOU DO TO BE
## committed to the change
## YOU WANT TO CREATE?

_____

_____

_____

_____

_____

_____

_____

_____

_____

_____

_____

_____

_____

_____

_____

_____

_____

_____

_____

Now, you're ready for the final ingredient in this rebel leader mix, devotion.

# BE DEVOTED TO YOUR PEOPLE

As I wrote about Beto O'Rourke, you probably noticed that he goes to great lengths to be there for his people, to listen to and support them in the change that each person wants to see in government. Going to talk to people in counties he had no chance of winning shows he is devoted to them.

**Rebel leaders prioritize devotion to their fans and followers.**

Recently, I was watching the Amazon television show *Red Oaks*. Set in the 1980s, it's a super funny, edgy trip down nostalgia avenue. In one episode, two of the characters were working out to Richard Simmons' *Sweatin' to the Oldies*. It was actually the same *Sweatin' to the Oldies* videotape (yep, a VHS tape) I had when I was growing up. I knew that tape so well. I loved it and I loved Richard Simmons.

What I loved about Richard Simmons is that he created a movement around fitness in the '80s that was so different than anything that existed at the time, going way beyond Jane Fonda with her perfect body and her leg warmers.

He created a space where *fitness was for everyone* regardless of shape or size. People who were sweating with Simmons felt like they belonged to something bigger than themselves. He promised and delivered a transformation for people for a better life, for a healthier life with more movement.

Even though I was a fan, there was something about him I didn't know until I listened to the podcast *Missing Richard Simmons*. Through the podcast, I found out that Richard Simmons was devoted to his people. Whether you were paying for one of his cruises or just going to an event, Simmons cared about you.

He would spend Sundays calling people and checking in to see how they were doing with their transformation. Could he be of service? What advice could he give them? Could he just listen to their struggles?

Wow! Who does that, right? Richard Simmons did. He was devoted to his people and committed to helping them change.

And hey, in turn, were devoted to him, his message, and his business.

> REBEL LEADERS ARE DEVOTED
> TO THE PEOPLE WHO RAISE THEIR
> HAND, SAY YES, AND TAKE ACTION.

So this begs the question, **how can you be more devoted to your audience and the people that you serve?**

How can you show up in a bigger way that shows you as the change maker? How can you be dedicated to your audience and the changes they are making?

Now, you don't have to call everyone individually like Richard Simmons did (in fact the podcast explained that the practice impacted his mental health), but you could take the approach that Mel Robbins does with #5SecondRule: she follows up with people who use the hashtag on social media and congratulates them on the change that they're making in their lives. That is devotion.

I'm always experimenting with new ways to be devoted. For example, I feature my clients on my podcast. If I see a media opportunity for a client, I forward it along. I introduce people to hosts of podcasts that I've been on. I like to be there for my people.

Take a moment to brainstorm:

## HOW CAN YOU BE MORE
## *devoted to the people*
## AND THE ORGANIZATIONS THAT YOU SERVE?

_____

_____

_____

_____

_____

_____

_____

_____

_____

Devotion is a requirement when you're a leader. The more devoted you are, the more devoted your people are. When you show your followers that you truly care about them and their success, they care about you and your success. They support your business and your movement and show up for you.

## INFLUENCE + CHANGE + DEVOTION = A MOVEMENT (AND A THRIVING BUSINESS)

When you have ethical influence, change, and devotion, they add up to the creation of a movement. You'll also create a thriving business that is about more than working the mythical four-hour work week or chasing the elusive seven-figure launch. You're creating something that has meaning.

When you embody leadership, you're also creating your legacy. Ripple effects of change will extend beyond your reach because of your work.

Now you're ready to embody the role of Rebel Leader. (If you're not ready yet, go take the "What's Your Rebel Roadmap to Exponential Impact + Influence?" Quiz at **www.therebelquiz.com**.) In the next chapter, I'll tell you exactly how creating a message that is bigger than your business benefits you, your people, and your industry.

**ADDITIONAL RESOURCE ALERT!**

# CHAPTER THREE:

## Why You Need a Message

# Bigger Than Your Business

**A**t this point, I know that I am asking a lot of you. I am asking you to step out and lead. I am asking you to start a movement. I am asking you to be very visible and even—gasp—famous.

Why am I asking for all of this?

Because I believe that your idea chose you. I believe that you wouldn't have picked up this book if you didn't have something brewing inside of you that needs to escape. Trust me, this idea of yours longs to get out. It longs to be heard, spoken, and spread. It chose you to be the messenger.

I realize that there are times when you hide out in the bathroom, shaking your fist in the air and asking, "Why did you choose me? Why me?" I know because I've been there.

When I first solidified this idea and named it the 3 Word Rebellion, there was a whisper that said, "This work is important and I choose you to do it." This idea—this 3 Word Rebellion—felt so big. It felt bigger than me. How was I going to pull this off? Why did I have to?

I remember being at dinner with my husband and sneaking off to the bathroom to wonder out loud, "Do I really have to do this?" The 3 Word Rebellion terrified me. I realized that this was the idea I'd be known for. It would have the power to launch a million rebellions. It would change everything for me.

And change is scary...oh so scary. After I had this major download, my next step was not to spring into action. My next step was to sleep! Yes, after having this *huge* epiphany I spent hours in bed sleeping. I didn't even tell my husband about the 3

Word Rebellion for a week. I just couldn't wrap my arms around the enormity of it all.

Once I was done sleeping and had told my husband about this idea over beers, I started quietly telling my coach and a few of my closest confidants and business besties. Each was like, "THIS IS AMAZING! GET TO WORK!"

I scheduled a webinar to introduce the 3 Word Rebellion because I wanted to be generous and get it into the hands of as many people as possible, as soon as possible.

What was my motivation to do all of this? I wanted to create a message that was bigger than me and bigger than my business. The 3 Word Rebellion is my legacy.

> YOUR 3 WORD REBELLION WILL BE YOUR LEGACY AS WELL.

Why on earth would I want to create a message bigger than my business? Why on Earth should you want the same?

Let's tackle two key points in order to fully answer these questions. Why is messaging important to your business? Why should you want a message that creates a movement?

# YOUR MESSAGE MATTERS
# MORE THAN YOU THINK

In the nine years that I've been in business, I noticed a curious phenomenon that happens in an online world. A business owner, let's call her Jessie, creates a great product or service. It sells based on word of mouth. The offering gets amazing results.

Now Jessie thinks, "This is awesome. I want to get this offer into the hands of more people. Change more lives and make more money. I need marketing."

She buys courses to teach her how to create a webinar that sells, takes a workshop in Instagram marketing, and hires a social media team so she can be visible on ALL the social media platforms.

Then nothing happens for Jessie. Her audience grows at the speed of sloths. She works hard to find anyone who is interested in hiring her. She's not making the impact she knows she can make with her work.

Finally, Jessie does what we've all done at one time or another. **She blames herself.** Jessie feels like she is craptastic at marketing and that's when the whole thing veers off course (and also when she is most susceptible to bro marketers promising to be the silver bullet that fixes all her business woes).

**Jessie's problem isn't the marketing. It's the messaging!**

During my brief stint in Corporate America, I managed a top-secret market research project for Microsoft. I'm not even sure I can tell you to this day what product it was because I promised my firstborn cat if I ever told.

Before the launch of this product, Microsoft spent a couple of million dollars testing the messaging. Because companies like Microsoft, Apple, and Nike know that it doesn't matter how good a product is if you don't know how to powerfully COMMUNICATE the value of the offer and build desire for it.

In fact, these huge corporations have brand message guides for each product in their company so every employee, contractor, and even the c-suite executives know how to talk about the products.

What does this mean for Jessie and you and your business? Well, it doesn't mean that you need to spend millions of dollars on message testing, but it does mean you need to develop a way to communicate the value and build desire for your offer.

Most of the marketing and business courses sold by the celebrity business owners give you swipes and almost done-for-you email templates chock-full of Bro Marketing tactics so that you don't spend time creating your messaging.

What happens? The swipes don't work as well as promised. The done-for-you emails result in zero sales because they are not aligned and make you sound like every other business owner on Planet Earth.

It doesn't work; not because the marketing tactic was bad—it doesn't work because your messaging is not aligned.

Your message powers all your sales and marketing. It's the **foundation of the copy** on your website, and those words are why people stick around and click around. Your message **compels people to sign up for your community**. It's what you write in social media posts that gets people to actually respond to them (what a concept). Your message is what you talk about on podcasts, on stages, or during a webinar.

Your message has three main missions. Capture Attention. Create Conversation. Cultivate Connection. I call these the A.C.C. way.

Let's talk about each aspect of The A.C.C. Way in more detail.

## ATTENTION

Did you know that your attention span is shorter than that of a goldfish? A goldfish pays attention for nine seconds and you and I only have eight-second attention spans. This is according to a study commissioned by Microsoft in 2020. You know what's even worse? On mobile, our attention span is only 4-seconds.

That means when your next client is scrolling Instagram, you've only got four precious seconds to make an impression— otherwise, they keep on scrolling. Do you feel that pressure?

Deep breath. The 3 Word Rebellion has your back. The purpose of a 3 Word Rebellion is to capture your right person's attention and make them curious to know more. The 3 Word Rebellion is the keystone of all your other messaging because if you can't capture attention, then you can't have a conversation or establish a connection with your audience.

# CONVERSATION

Once you capture someone's attention and they're curious to know more, the second mission of your message begins. It's time to create conversation. They are human. You're human. **All marketing is one human being talking to another.**

This person who is interested in your message and your business has questions. She must decide if your business is right for her. Your job is to answer these questions by creating a Client Journey that gets people to fully buy into your 3 Word Rebellion, your work, and to hire you to help them. There are certain decisions that your potential clients need to make before they act on your message. I call these messaging marks, as in "Is your message hitting the mark?"

I'll go into this in more depth in Chapter 8. Once we start engaging, answering questions, and helping people decide, a wonderful thing happens—connection.

# CONNECTION

Unless you're dwelling under a rock, you've heard all about the know, like, and trust factor. You've got to have this if you want people to follow you and buy from you. Your 3 Word Rebellion and your Client Decision Journey do more than create the know, like, and trust factor—it cultivates empathy.

We create empathy through the Signature Stories we tell. People just want to feel like they belong. People want to feel seen and heard. They want to know that you get them...like really, truly, deeply understand. You understand their experience. You empathize with their problems (not poke at their pain points), and you have a solution to help them.

Yes, we establish connection during the Client Journey, but the most powerful way to do that is through telling a story. Your story. Your clients' stories. Heck, even research can be a story. The story is how the right person for your business and movement SEES themself in what you're creating. We'll be talking more about the story in Chapter 8.

Your messaging powers everything you do in your business. It's how you capture attention, create conversations, and cultivate connection. When you know how to communicate in a way that accomplishes these three missions, everything becomes easier in your business. I promise. This is the reason I'm writing this book to give you a message that matters.

## MESSAGING + MARKETING
## = MORE MONEY & IMPACT

You're here to do more than make money, right? You are a rebel on the rise who is here to make a difference. You want impact! You're seeing how your message matters in your business, but I get it—you need a bit of convincing and a pep talk to go all in on this concept of building a movement around your business! Here are three good reasons to start a movement with your message.

# REASON #1:
# YOUR MOVEMENT GIVES PEOPLE
# A PLACE TO BELONG

When people take action on your message, they begin to change. They don't just change their behavior. They begin to change their identity. This is huge: they actually evolve and become someone new because of your message (how cool is that?). When we start changing *who* we are at our core, we need a place to belong. Your movement creates a safe place for that evolution to occur.

The students from Parkland, Florida, who started the #NeverAgain movement are a constant inspiration to me. Within their movement, they created a place for students to speak out and express their fears and safety concerns about going to school every day. In that space they are banding together to get out the vote and make changes to gun laws in the United States so that *all* students can feel safe in school.

Black Lives Matter is a movement that provides a place where people of color can come together to fight oppression and violence by the dominant white culture. In that space, they can call out abuses of power and systemic violence by the police and others.

These social movements started because of trauma. However, a 3 Word Rebellion movement that creates a place of belonging doesn't have to spring from heartache and devastation; it can also start with something fun.

This may seem nonsensical, but I think rock bands do this very well. Since I was eight years old, I have been obsessed with the '80s band Duran Duran. When I was younger the walls of my bedroom were adorned with the faces of Simon, John, Nick, Roger, and Andy. I loved them (and Simon the most). During my rather tumultuous childhood, that band was there for me. Their music sang me to sleep almost every single night.

When I was in my early 30s I found myself with disposal income at the time my favorite band was doing a reunion tour. I started traveling the U.S.—and the globe—to see Duran Duran in concert. When I did, I found more than just amazing concerts, I found my people.

The people I met were outsiders like me. They suffered from a childhood trauma like me. The band helped them navigate that trauma just like me. The band created a place where I belonged. A place that was safe to discuss what had happened in the past and how Duran Duran had shone a light through the drama.

Duran Duran created a safe place for me to belong and find my people.

I believe that Mel Robbins creates a place of belonging for her people as well. She created a place for them to share how they are taking action and evolving into a better version of themselves. Where they can take big scary action and talk about it online. Where they know that taking the action is the important step and not the outcome. They have a safe place to fail and Mel and her crew will be there to support them.

When we have a message that calls people in, we create a place for them to belong and do the work that must be done to move forward.

Take a moment and answer this question:

## WHAT ARE THE VALUES THAT UNDERLY YOUR MOVEMENT?

What are the experiences that connect people in your movement?

_____
_____
_____
_____
_____
_____
_____
_____
_____
_____
_____
_____
_____
_____
_____
_____
_____
_____

# REASON #2:
# YOUR PEOPLE BECOME
# THE PROTECTORS AND DEFENDERS
# OF YOUR MOVEMENT

When people feel like they belong and have a safe space for transformation, they then feel like they have an ownership stake in what you created. When they don't have a stake in your movement or your business, they walk away when you need them most.

Tony Robbins found this out the hard way in 2018 when he decided to take on the #MeToo movement at one of his events.

In case you don't know about Robbins' kerfuffle, here's a quick recap from writer Maiysha Kai:

In the clip, which was taped at a March 15 seminar in San Jose, Calif., Robbins gave his (likely unasked for and certainly unhelpful) opinion on the #MeToo movement. In the process, he suggested that those who identify with it were engaged in "victimhood" while trying to gain "significance," and that even righteous "anger is not empowerment."

Even as criticism swelled up around him, Robbins was adamant that he would not apologize. He believed that his point of view was the correct one and that the people he was leading would fall in line.

Except they did not rise up to protect him and no one seemed to defend his viewpoint. I didn't hear a peep from his super fans and his supporters about this event. In the end, the heat Robbins was under was too intense and he was forced to apologize (although I question how sincere an apology is when one is forced to make it).

Tony Robbins had to apologize because what he lacks, the #MeToo movement has in abundance. Yes, Robbins has power and influence. Money galore. Millions of fans. But the #MeToo movement has millions of women who identify with it and what it is striving to do. When women use #MeToo, they are raising their hands to say, "I am a survivor" and "It's time this violence against women ends."

> WHEN PEOPLE IDENTIFY WITH YOUR MESSAGE AND RAISE THEIR HAND TO SAY, "YES, I BELONG HERE," THE MESSAGE BECOMES A PART OF WHO THEY ARE. THE MESSAGE BECOMES BIGGER THAN YOUR BUSINESS.

When that happens, they become the protectors of your message. They defend the message because the movement has created a space where they belong.

But Robbins built a business for Robbins. As a result, his legions of fans don't identify with what he's created. His fans are simply paying customers and don't feel a part of something more. Despite his money, power, and fame, Tony Robbins has failed to build a message bigger than himself and his business. And when he stepped in it, his people were not there to support him.

> DON'T BUILD YOUR BUSINESS FOR YOU. BUILD YOUR BUSINESS FOR THE PEOPLE WHO ARE CHANGED BY YOUR 3 WORD REBELLION.

Challenging the status quo is tough work. It's lonely work. People will resist the change you are trying to create. They may even attack you. But when you have people who are a part of what you have created and feel like they belong to it, they will come to your defense and support your vision.

An example of this can be seen in what occurred when Fox News personality Laura Ingraham decided to personally attack David Hogg, one of the survivors of the school shooting in Parkland, Florida, for not getting into the colleges of his choice. In response, Hogg took to Twitter and told the members of the #NeverAgain movement that this was unacceptable behavior and to go after Ingraham where it would hurt the most: her advertisers. As of this writing, Laura Ingraham has lost 24 sponsors of her show. Hogg's Twitter followers took action because they believe in the movement and the message, not just in Hogg. They believe in schools where children feel safe. They believe in the gun control he advocates for.

These examples show the power of belonging that your followers feel when you have a movement standing behind you. That feeling of being apart of group allows them to take action together. Your followers become the protectors and defenders of your movement because they identify with it.

Now, it's time to dream.

# WHAT DO YOU WANT PEOPLE WHO ARE A PART OF YOUR MOVEMENT *to do?*

_____

_____

_____

_____

_____

_____

_____

_____

_____

_____

_____

_____

_____

_____

_____

_____

_____

_____

_____

# HOW DO YOU WANT THEM TO
## protect and defend the message?

_____

_____

_____

_____

_____

_____

_____

_____

_____

_____

_____

_____

_____

_____

_____

_____

_____

_____

_____

_____

_____

_____

# REASON #3:
# YOUR MESSAGE TAKES ON
# A LIFE OF ITS OWN

This final reason is the scariest reason to make your message bigger than you or your business: the message takes on a life of its own beyond just you.

I know this 3 Word Rebellion that you are creating is important to you. It feels like your baby that you're birthing, supporting, and helping grow into adulthood. You've invested your money, your time, and your energy in giving it life, and now I'm asking you to set it free.

Yes, that's exactly what I am asking you to do: pour your heart, soul, sweat, tears, and dollars into it and then let it go. This is your legacy and it is what you'll always be remembered for. If you want to make a lasting difference to people, you have to allow people to steward your message without your input.

Simon Sinek is a beautiful example of this. His TEDx talk "How Great Leaders Inspire Action," based on the very simple premise that companies who succeed beyond expectations know their why, went viral.

He didn't plan it, but Start with Why became a cultural phenomenon. Everyone was wondering what their why was and how to find it. More importantly, we started talking to each other about our whys. Now, when you get burned out on your business, people tell you to go back to your why. They might even hand you Sinek's book and tell you to dive in.

Businesses cropped up that would coach you to find your why. I heard speakers talk about Start with Why in their presentations. (Sidenote: Always cite your sources, people. I hate seeing "start with why" on a sales page or in a speech with no mention of Sinek's name. Give credit where credit is due, yo!)

Start with Why became so much bigger than Sinek that there was no way he could personally help all the people who were interested in his work. His message became bigger than him. His followers took up the mantle of acting on and talking about Start with Why. His 3 Word Rebellion lives and breathes without him until this very day.

The cool part is that this has allowed him to evolve his own work. He has been able to write books on leadership and talk about topics other than your why and the related Golden Circle. His movement still grows and he as a leader still evolves. This is the best part of your message taking on a life of its own. You can still grow, evolve, and work on other things without being tethered to what you created.

**Take a moment and journal here on this question:**

# IMAGINE POURING YOUR HEART, SOUL, TIME AND ENERGY INTO CRAFTING YOUR 3 WORD REBELLION.

## How would it feel...

# IF OTHER PEOPLE WERE TALKING ABOUT YOUR 3 WORD REBELLION? HOW WOULD IT FEEL IF OTHER PEOPLE WERE TALKING ABOUT YOUR 3 WORD REBELLION AND NOT MENTIONING YOU AS THE CREATOR? HOW CAN YOU PREPARE TO LET IT GO?

_____

_____

_____

_____

_____

_____

_____

_____

_____

The goal of this chapter is to convince you that you *do* want to create a movement with your message. When you create a movement, you create a space of belonging, you cultivate protectors and defenders of the message, and you create your own legacy.

What do I want you to take away from all of this?

I want you to think bigger. Create a message that is bigger than you, your speaking career, and your business.

Create a battle cry that people can say yes to. A space where people feel like they belong. Allow your message to be bigger than you and it will take on a life of its own.

This is why I want you to have a 3 Word Rebellion.

The 3 Word Rebellion calls in your people, incites them to act, and gives them a place to belong. It encourages them to be the keepers and protectors of your message.

That is when the magic happens. This is how you make an impact. This is how you create a legacy.

Now that you know *why* you should create a movement with your message, you're ready to start to craft your 3 Word Rebellion in the next chapter.

# CHAPTER FOUR

# Questions that Lead to a Rebellion

**L**et's get down to it. How do you create your 3 Word Rebellion?

You find it by writing. This chapter is going to give you thoughtful and enjoyable prompts for exploring your business, your passions, and your industry. If you haven't written in the book yet (this Book is sad and wants to interact with you), it's time to get out a pen and sully these pristine pages with your heartfelt thoughts and ideas.

## REMEMBER, YOUR 3 WORD REBELLION ALREADY EXISTS.

It's just waiting for you to get your hands dirty and dig it out. This is the time to get messy with your message (that's why it's called a *MESSage*). Believe that it exists and that you will find it by free writing.

So what is free writing? It is a technique where you set aside a chunk of time and write continuously. This approach helps you overcome your overthinking about your message, busts through your writer's block, and tells your inner critic to shut its piehole.

Free writing allows you to say what you want to say. Put it all out there without censoring yourself. No judgment. No worries about what others will think if you say what is in your heart. There are no right or wrong answers. You don't have to be grammatically correct, be politically correct, or even spell correctly. You just have to free your mind and write.

I guarantee you that this will produce a fair amount of brilliance and garbage. There's value in both. Simply, free writing gives you raw data. Yes, I want you to look at what you write like a scientist would view an experiment. How an ethnographer approaches studying a new culture. It's data. I'll be talking more about this point of view in Chapter Five (spoiler alert: research is in my blood), but viewing your words as data points allows you to detach from the outcome.

I want you to get over yourself, stop thinking so much, and stop worrying about being right. There's no right here! Ready? Onward!

## WHAT ARE YOU REBELLING AGAINST?

The first part of finding your 3 Word Rebellion is knowing what you are rebelling against. If you find the status quo hunky dory (why did you buy this book?), then you need to find a different framework for your message because this isn't the one for you.

IF YOU DON'T THINK YOU'RE
A REBEL BECAUSE YOU THINK
YOU'RE A CREATOR OR INNOVATOR
AND JUST WANT THE WORLD
TO BE BETTER PLACE,
HERE'S A REBEL TRUTH:

# YOU MUST
# DESTROY
# IN ORDER
# TO CREATE.

Two competing systems cannot exist at the same time. A country can't be both communist and capitalist. You can't have patriarchy and matriarchy at the same time.

I spent the first six years of my business working with speakers who wanted to be paid for their work. I realized the premier organization for paid speakers, the National Speakers Association, does not pay the speakers for their conference. An industry cannot both value speakers getting paid and not pay their speakers. That paradigm must be destroyed in order for a new system to rise.

You have to challenge the status quo. You've got to tear down what you don't like in order to build something new. This is your opportunity to admit what ticks you off and how you would like your industry, society, or even the world to be different.

> ALL MOVEMENTS ARE MOVING AWAY FROM SOMETHING IN THE STATUS QUO.

The starting point to finding your 3 Word Rebellion and starting a movement with your message is to figure out what you're moving away from.

You can want to see change on at least one of three different levels:

* Societal
* Industry
* Personal

On the societal level, The #NeverAgain movement is moving away from guns being so accessible that anyone can buy them and use them in a classroom. Black Lives Matter wants society to move away from black people being shot by the police more than any other race. Make America Great Again wants to go backward to a mythical time when America was great (great for straight white men...more on that in Chapter Five).

On the industry level, Simon Sinek is rebelling against joyless, purposeless, soul-sucking businesses. I've been rebelling against the speaking industry for how they compensate speakers.

Finally, many of the speakers that I greatly admire, their work is moving away from a status quo they want to change on the personal level: Mel Robbins is rebelling against the status quo in individuals lives (how meta of her). Sally Hogshead is rebelling against people being boring.

Now it's time to write about what you're rebelling against. Rant. Rave. Just let it all out. If you have a physical copy of this book in your hot hands, grab your pen (and an optional glass of wine or pint of beer) and answer the following questions in the book. If you don't want to write in the book, go get the 3 Word Rebellion toolkit at **drmichellemazur.com/download** to grab the prompts in PDF form and print those out. Then go to town on the following three questions.

**ADDITIONAL RESOURCE ALERT!**

I recommend setting a timer for about 30 minutes and just letting it flow. Don't know how to start? Write "I don't know what to say" over and over again like Bart Simpson during the opening of *The Simpsons*. Eventually the words will come. Don't like to write? Hit record on your phone, answer out loud, and get it transcribed.

Here are three free-writing prompts to help you get clear on what you want to change:

WHAT ARE YOU
## rebelling against?

_____
_____
_____
_____
_____
_____
_____
_____
_____
_____
_____
_____

_____

_____

_____

_____

_____

_____

_____

_____

_____

_____

_____

_____

_____

_____

_____

_____

_____

_____

_____

_____

_____

_____

_____

_____

_____

# It pisses me off

## WHEN...

_____

_____

_____

_____

_____

_____

_____

_____

_____

_____

_____

_____

_____

_____

_____

_____

_____

_____

_____

_____

_____

_____

_____

_____

_____

_____

_____

_____

_____

_____

_____

_____

_____

_____

_____

_____

_____

_____

_____

_____

_____

_____

_____

_____

_____

_____

_____

_____

_____

# It hurts my heart

## WHEN...

_____
_____
_____
_____
_____
_____
_____
_____
_____
_____
_____
_____
_____
_____
_____
_____
_____
_____
_____
_____

_____

_____

_____

_____

_____

_____

_____

_____

_____

_____

_____

_____

_____

_____

_____

_____

_____

# Congratulations!

## YOU'VE REBELLED AGAINST THE STATUS QUO.

## LET'S KEEP GOING WITH THE FUN.

# WHAT'S THE CHANGE
# YOU WANT TO CREATE?

A rebellion is *not* a riot. It's not chaos. It's not saying this sucks, it needs to change, and then shirking off the responsibility to create something new.

> POINTING OUT WHAT'S WRONG WITHOUT MAKING THE SPACE TO USHER IN THE NEW IS COMPLAINING.

Remember, movements like Occupy Wall Street failed because while the rebellion was clear, the change was not. Income inequality sucks. It does. But while this movement was crystal clear on what needed to change, they didn't have a clear vision of what they wanted to replace the flawed financial system with.

When you destroy a system, a way of being, or an industry, you must have a vision to replace it or one of two things happens. Either the movement fizzles like we saw with Occupy Wall Street, or the system you're rebelling against gets replaced with something far worse.

Here's the opportunity. *You* get to create that vision of the world you want to live in, whether it's for your audience, for your industry, or even society. It's time for you to be the creator, the innovator, the visionary that leads your people to a better place. This is why before I give you these prompts, I want you to make this mindset shift.

# FORGET THE HOW.
# FOCUS ON THE WHAT IF.

As you answer the following prompts, I don't want you to worry about the how. How thinking is a trap that keeps you from envisioning something better. How thinking keeps you stuck in the status quo. Frankly, the how is not your issue right now. You get to figure out the how with the people who are raising their hand and saying yes to the vision you want to create.

Instead, focus on what if thinking. What if opens you up to possibility. What if allows you to co-create new solutions. What if allows you to evolve that vision as new ideas emerge.

Are you down with the what if? Excellent!

Your journey to creating this world starts by answering the three questions below.

The same rules apply here. Don't censor yourself. Write. Let it flow out of you. Don't care about grammar, spelling, or if it even makes sense. And of course wine or craft beer is recommended (if that's your thing).

You're about to starting laying the groundwork for changing your audience, your industry, and the world. Set a timer for 30 minutes and let it flow.

# What change

## DO YOU WANT TO CREATE?

_____

_____

_____

_____

_____

_____

_____

_____

_____

_____

_____

_____

_____

_____

_____

_____

_____

_____

_____

_____

_____

_____

_____

_____

_____

_____

_____

_____

# I want to live

## IN A WORLD WHERE...

_____
_____
_____
_____
_____
_____
_____
_____
_____
_____
_____
_____
_____
_____
_____
_____
_____
_____
_____
_____

_____

_____

_____

_____

_____

_____

_____

_____

_____

_____

_____

_____

_____

_____

_____

_____

_____

_____

_____

_____

_____

_____

_____

_____

_____

_____

_____

# IF EVERYONE ACTED
# ON YOUR MESSAGE,
## what would the world be like?

(I always get teary when I hear my clients' answers to this one.)

_____

_____

_____

_____

_____

_____

_____

_____

_____

_____

_____

_____

_____

_____

_____

_____

_____

_____

_____
_____
_____
_____
_____
_____
_____
_____
_____
_____
_____
_____
_____
_____
_____
_____
_____
_____
_____

# Congratulations!

## YOU'VE DONE ALL THE WRITING FOR YOUR 3 WORD REBELLION

*(THE BOOK WANTS ME TO TELL YOU HOW HAPPY IT IS THAT YOU WROTE IN IT...IT FEELS GOOD).*

Before you continue to the next section, go look at how much you wrote for the rebellion questions and then look at how much you wrote for the change section. If you wrote more for the rebellion questions than for the change freewriting section, stop and revisit the change prompts. Elaborate more on the change your work creates. For each sentence you wrote, ask yourself "Why?" Why does that change matter? What will it do for my clients, my community, and even the world? Go deeper.

Most 3 Word Rebellions come from the change you want to create section, so spend time here dreaming about the possibilities and your impact.

If you wrote about the same for these two sections or wrote a novel about the way the world could be, then it's time for the next step before you create your 3 Word Rebellion...

## AN ETHICS CHECK

You didn't think I would forget about ethics, did you?

Now that you have a clear idea of the change or changes that you want to create, it's time to consider the ethical implications.

Take some time to respond to the following questions:

## HOW IS THIS CHANGE
# *going to impact*
## PEOPLE DIRECTLY?

_____
_____
_____
_____

## HOW IS IT
# *going to change*
## YOUR INDUSTRY AND SOCIETY?

_____
_____
_____
_____

COULD THERE BE ANY
## unintended consequences
THAT WOULD HARM PEOPLE
FURTHER?

_____

_____

_____

_____


DO YOU FEEL THAT THIS CHANGE
IS IN YOUR AUDIENCE'S
## best interests,
NOT JUST YOUR OWN?

_____

_____

_____

_____

What if you didn't pass the ethics check? I'd ask you to go back through what you wrote and see what needs to be eliminated or added so that the rebellion that you're creating can be good for your people. Don't move on to the next step until the ethics are in check!

If you're feeling great about how your change impacts others, the next step is to begin writing your 3 Word Rebellion.

But first it is time for a PAUSE.

Let your writing sit and percolate overnight. Don't edit it or do anything else with it. Put down this book *now* and go watch Netflix or Hulu or listen to a comedian on Spotify. Before you go, block out some time in your calendar tomorrow or the day after to come back to this. That's when we are going to start crafting your 3 Word Rebellion with the help of the next chapter.

# CHAPTER FIVE

# Crafting Your 3 Word Rebellion

**Y**ou've done the free writing. You've let it sit overnight (or longer, as percolation doesn't always happen quickly). Now, you're ready to start writing your 3 Word Rebellion.

This is the most critical part of the whole process. When you nail your 3 Word Rebellion, you will gather your people who say yes to the change you want to create. When they say yes and experience that change for themselves, they will start to spread your message. If those people don't understand your 3 Word Rebellion or don't resonate with what you've said, they won't feel compelled to join you.

I WANT TO LAY ONE BIG
REBEL TRUTH ON YOU
BEFORE WE BEGIN:

# MESSAGING
# IS
# HARD!

Why do you think Bro Marketers are so successful in recruiting people to that way of messaging and marketing? It's easier than doing the in-depth work of finding your message. Finding the right words that people respond to and are persuaded by is one of the most difficult things you will ever do as a movement maker, speaker, or business owner.

It's challenging and worth it. Once you find the right words, a cascade effect occurs. Your right people resonate and understand your message, and that makes showing up to market your business, grow your audience, and sell your life-changing offers exponentially easier. Plus, it lays the whole foundation for how you communicate in your business, making copywriting easier and marketing a breeze. Hang in there. It's worth it!

I've worked with people who have been struggling for months (or even years) with figuring out their message. When they figure out their message, they feel RELIEF! If you've struggled with messaging before, rest assured that you're not alone, there are good reasons for it, and there's something you can do about it! Sweet relief is on the way.

## WHY IS FINDING YOUR MESSAGE A STRUGGLE?

The first reason it's a struggle to find your message is that you are cursed—cursed with knowledge. You are way too close to your own message to see it clearly and to approach it with a beginner's mindset. On a scale from 1 to 10, with 1 being you know nothing about the topic and 10 being you are an absolute expert on the topic, you are an 11.

Your audience is at a 1 or 2. That's a huge gap to close. During my 25 years of working with business owners of all types, I've noticed that when an entrepreneur feels like they are bringing it down to the audience's level, their expertise rating is still at a 6 or 7. That is still a ginormous gap!

This means that the business owner is still assuming that the audience has a level of expertise with the message that they don't have. This creates confusion. The audience doesn't get it. The message feels out of their league (or worse, they feel stupid). When your message does not connect with the audience on the level of their own knowledge and experience, they walk away from you and the change you want to create.

Another reason messaging is tough is that while you're thinking about the message that changes the world and that you want to be known for, you also need to be thinking about how your audience will receive that message. Will they understand it? What (if any) resistance is there to that message? This is why it's also critical to get feedback along the way.

Here's an example of what I mean. A few years ago, I had a consult with a would-be client who wanted me to help her market her speaking. (The details have been changed to protect the innocent.) She had been working *hard* on her message. She was so proud of what she'd created. She had come up with two clever acronyms that described her whole framework for how she was going to change the nonprofit world for the good.

I could tell she'd been working too hard for too long without any feedback. Those two clever acronyms didn't make any sense to me. In fact, when she proudly told me what her message was, it sounded like she wanted to bring religion to the sex industry.

Then I broke her heart and gave her the feedback that she should have gotten months before if only she had talked to someone with a critical eye who was willing to tell her the real truth: No one in her intended audience was going to understand this message. It needed a better hook in order to catch on. What she'd come up with was just too clever.

## CLEVER IS THE ENEMY OF CLARITY...ALWAYS!

Remember this as you go through the process.

Now that we are on the same page that messaging is tough, creative work and we need to get feedback on it, I would like to make a few suggestions:

* Take the first pass at doing the analysis I describe below and writing your 3 Word Rebellion on your own. Then get help if you haven't nailed it.

* Find a friend in the rebellion. Choose someone who understands who you want to lead in your movement, can think about your message the way your audience would, and can give you feedback. Give them a copy of this book and do this work together. Or join me for a 3 Word Rebellion Messaging Intensive to get my help and be with other change makers like you working to craft their message.

* **Don't go it alone or your message will stay a mess.** Don't talk to your friends and family who just want you to be happy; they won't give you good feedback. Don't ask the

people who already think that you shit unicorns and glitter. You want a person with a discerning eye.

Let's get on with how to analyze (oh yes, I did say analyze) your free writing. This writing holds the ingredients that will make up your 3 Word Rebellion.

## GET NERDY WITH IT: VIEW YOUR WORDS AS DATA

I have a Ph.D. in communication, which means I'm a researcher at heart. My top strength on the Strengths Finder® isn't Communication (that's number two), but Input, which is all about gathering information. I was trained in both qualitative and quantitative methods. One lesson that I learned from conducting research studies in academia and market research studies for Fortune 500 companies is *objectivity*.

When researchers analyze data, they bring (to the best of their ability) objectivity to the data set. They may have a hypothesis or a hunch on what the data will tell them, but they let the data itself tell the story. They don't manipulate the data to tell the story that they want to tell (well, some researchers do—especially in studies sponsored by special interest groups who have a vested interest in the findings…but I digress).

Now, I'm sure you didn't expect to get a research lesson in this book. But objectivity is essential for you in crafting your 3 Word Rebellion. Being objective means looking at what you wrote in the free write with detachment. Analyzing your writing without any preconceived notions. Detach from the words.

DETACH FROM WHAT YOU THINK YOUR 3 WORD REBELLION SHOULD BE. DETACH FROM WHAT YOU THINK IS POPULAR OR WHAT OTHER PEOPLE ARE SAYING.

**Be a scientist. Be a researcher. View your words with a discerning eye.**

Now to go further down the research rabbit hole, I want you to view each word as a separate data point.

## WHAT CLUES TO LOOK FOR IN YOUR WRITING

I'm going to share with you the same process I use when I analyze my clients' free writes. First, I read through the free writing just to get a general understanding of my client and their audience. Then I read it a second time, looking for clues in the writing. The third and final time, I read through it backwards, starting with the last question and finishing with the first. This final pass through allows me to see the writing from a different perspective and reveals clues that I might have missed.

What clues should you be looking for during those second and third reads? You want to look for action verbs (no "being" verbs like *is, be, was, were,* etc.). Interesting nouns. Standout turns of phrase. Words that grab your attention.

You also want to look for themes. Do you notice any patterns? Were there any thoughts repeated multiple times? These themes and patterns can clue you in to what your 3 Word Rebellion wants to be.

If you want to see a video of how I approach the analysis and get a checklist of how to do this analysis, head over to **drmichellemazur.com/download** to grab

**ADDITIONAL** the 3 Word Rebellion Toolkit.

**RESOURCE**       **Confession time: About once every three months, I**

**ALERT!**            **do the exercises in this book to see how my message is evolving or changing.** Sometimes I do this activity and not much has changed in my viewpoints. Other times, I do this writing and everything changes. My 3 Word Rebellion has changed over the years (more on that later in this chapter). I find new ideas and new ways to communicate and share my ideas.

Here's a free write that I did for my own business when I was still working with speakers. (The summary here is an amalgamation of my responses to all six questions.)

* The speaking industry doesn't want to pay you
* Good speakers with good intentions damage their brand with lousy messages
* Focus on changing your audience
* Be fiercely devoted to your audience
* Shake up the status quo—REBEL
* If you're a speaker, then you're a leader—so LEAD!
* No, really, your speech/your message is not about you
* Stir shit up, challenge your audience and lead them to a better way
* Incite action always

* Don't spread an idea—change your audience

There was so much more I wrote down, but I'll leave it at that. Now, if I were my own client, I'd be patting myself on the back for making such a wise investment. Then during my second and third read-throughs, I would highlight the verbs, nouns, and turns of phrase that stand out.

* The **speaking industry** doesn't want to pay you
* Good speakers with good **intentions damage** their **brand** with **lousy** messages
* **Focus** on **changing** your **audience**
* Be **fiercely devoted** to your audience
* Shake up the status quo—**REBEL**
* If you're a speaker, then you're a **leader**—so **LEAD!**
* No, really, your speech/your message is not about you
* **Stir** shit up, **challenge** your audience and lead them to a better way
* **Incite action always**
* Don't **spread** an **idea**—**change** your audience

Then based on these words, I would create a word bank like this:

* Speaking industry
* Intentions
* Damage/Damaging
* Brand
* Focus
* Change/Changing
* Fiercely devoted
* Rebel
* Leader/Lead

* Stir
* Challenge
* Incite action always
* Idea
* Spread

I will say that as I look over that list, there's one turn of phrase that stands out. I think "incite action always" is a pretty hot 3 Word Rebellion. It's positioned against TED's "ideas worth spreading" and even has some nice alliteration.

I could stop here and be happy. But what if there is something better waiting for me? It's worth it for me to detach and move on to the next step, right? "Incite action always" will be here waiting for me, but I owe it to myself and the people that I want to change and the movement I want to create to keep on going.

But before I do, I want you to take your turn.

The first step is to turn back to the free writing exercises you completed on pages 66-86, get out your highlighter, look at the individual words, and highlight those nouns, action verbs, and turns of phrase that you find interesting.

Go on. I'll be waiting here for you when you get back.

Now that you've done the analysis, the second step is to create a list of words that you could use to formulate your 3 Word Rebellion.

If you feel like you're too attached or don't think any of your words pop, you've got two choices. Number one, let your writing sit for a couple more nights (almost so you forget what you wrote in the first place) and come back with fresh eyes. Or number two, do more writing. Write until you have nothing left to say.

HERE IN THE SPACE BELOW,
WRITE DOWN YOUR

# word bank for nouns/
# turns of phrase.

_____

_____

_____

_____

_____

_____

_____

_____

_____

_____

_____

_____

_____

_____

_____

_____

_____

_____

_____

_____

_____

_____

_____

# NEXT, WRITE DOWN YOUR
## word bank for verbs.

_____

_____

_____

_____

_____

_____

_____

_____

_____

_____

_____

_____

_____

_____

_____

_____

_____

_____

_____

_____

_____

_____

_____

Now to the rules of the 3 Word Rebellion. Yes, even a rebellion needs rules—or, as I like to think about it, creative constraints.

## THE "RULES" OF WRITING YOUR 3 WORD REBELLION

You've been through a creative process with the free write and an analytic process in creating your rebellion word bank. Now, you get to be creative again, but this time with some rules.

I know we are rebels and we like to break the rules. I know you want to shake up the status quo. But creativity without constraints leads to chaos.

It also leads to analysis paralysis, which leads to you not taking action and not moving forward with your message. That's when stewing begins. Frustration sets in. You start questioning, "Is this one word the right word or is it *that* word?"

If you've ever stared at a blinking cursor on a blank page or been told that you could talk about whatever you wanted for five minutes, you most likely felt the paralysis of choice that comes with being able to do whatever you want.

Constraints actually allow you to show up as your best creative self. They provide structure. They give you a starting place for writing your 3 Word Rebellion.

YES, THIS REBEL IS TELLING YOU RULES CAN SET YOU FREE!

Did you know that Dr. Seuss's editor challenged him to write a book using only 50 words? That seems impossible. But Dr. Seuss accepted that challenge and rose to it. Out of that creative constraint, one of Dr. Seuss's most loved books was born: *Green Eggs and Ham.*

Constraints force us to become more creative and to think differently. That's why I'm asking you to apply the four creative constraints outlined below while developing your 3 Word Rebellion.

**Bonus: These constraints will make for a better, more effective, more attention-getting 3 Word Rebellion in the end.**

# CREATIVE CONSTRAINT #1: CHOOSE YOUR FLAVOR OF 3 WORD REBELLION

When I started analyzing others' messages, I realized that there are three flavors of 3 Word Rebellions that social movements and successful businesses and speakers use. **There's the Battle Cry, Naming the Change, and the Declaration.**

The Battle Cry is a powerful command, whereas Naming the Change is about giving a name to the movement that you're creating or the agent that brings about change. Finally, the Declaration is a mantra-like statement about the result you're promising your clients. Let me elaborate further.

Sidenote: I encourage you to play and experiment with each type of 3 Word Rebellion as you move through this process.

# THE BATTLE CRY

The Battle Cry is a command, the rallying cry for your movement. It is a directive for your audience about the change that you want to create. It should be clear what next step the audience should take to bring about that change.

The Battle Cry always starts with an action verb. Since it is action oriented, it's the type of 3 Word Rebellion that leads to action.

Some examples of the Battle Cry:

* Start with Why (Simon Sinek)
* Make America Great Again (Donald Trump)
* Incite Action Always (my trial 3 Word Rebellion)

Let's analyze these Battle Cries.

Simon Sinek's Start with Why begins with a powerful verb telling the audience to *start* something, and what he wants them to do is find their why (their purpose for being in business). Start with Why was a very, very effective battle cry that started as a TEDx talk viewed by millions and a best-selling book, a devoted social media following, and a new perspective on how to view your business trajectory.

In Donald Trump's 2016 presidential campaign, his Battle Cry (as most of you well know) was Make America Great Again. This was a call to go back to an unspecified period of time when America was truly great. His supporters knew exactly what to do to make that happen: they had to vote for Donald Trump. And vote they did, as Trump became the 45th president of the United States.

I would be remiss if I didn't mention that this rallying cry also delineated the ingroup and out group for Trump's election. This Battle Cry was for white people. For people of color, LGBTQ+, women, and non-binary individuals, going back to a time when America was "great" would mean a time of oppression. A time when black people were not allowed to vote. A time when women couldn't get access to the healthcare they needed or even have a credit card. A time when LGBTQ+ people couldn't marry who they loved. A time when non-binary individuals had to hide who they are from the world.

Based on the results of the 2016 election, this strategy worked. People of color voted overwhelmingly for Secretary Hillary Clinton. According to fivethirtyeight.com, statistician Nate Silver's site, 63% of white men voted for Trump and 53% of white women voted for Trump. Contrast that number to 88% of all African Americans voting for Clinton and 93% of black women voting for Clinton.

Trump's Battle Cry worked because it called in the exact people he needed for his movement (and yes, it's okay if your 3 Word Rebellion has four words—more on this below). I would also mention that this Battle Cry shows how powerful the 3 Word Rebellion is and how harmful it is when a leader goes down an unethical path with their rhetoric.

Finally, from my free writing, Incite Action Always is a potential 3 Word Rebellion. Why does this work? *Incite* is a powerful verb. It's also unexpected, as it's not a commonly used word. And it tells the audience what I want them to do with their message so they know the exact next step to take.

# NAMING THE CHANGE

Naming the Change is about either giving a name to the change you want to create or calling out the agent of change itself. A 3 Word Rebellion that names the change is typically but not necessarily a noun.

Some examples of Naming the Change:

* 5 Second Rule (Mel Robbins)
* Black Lives Matter
* 3 Word Rebellion

Let's analyze these Naming the Change examples.

The 5 Second Rule is an awesome example of naming the agent of change (the 5 Second Rule is *how* people take action). This message also drives curiosity. If you hear about the 5 Second Rule, you want to know what it is. Then when you find out that the rule is about counting backwards from five and taking an action, it's memorable. Anytime you feel stuck, you remember the 5 Second Rule, use it, and get unstuck.

Black Lives Matter is a powerful example of the change that a movement wants to create. It's simple. It's easy to grasp. It's a reminder of all the black men and women who have been shot and killed. It's about making black lives matter. You know exactly what change this group wants to create in the world.

Finally, 3 Word Rebellion is another great example of naming the change. It makes people curious; they want to know what it is. Then they want to know what theirs is. It incites them to create a message that is bigger than their business.

# THE DECLARATION

The declaration is a promise. It promises the result or change that your client can experience when they engage with your content and your work. It's a phrase that people could easily repeat to themselves, reminding them of the result they are seeking.

Some examples of The Declaration:

* Profit without Worry (Michelle Evans)
* Everything is Figureoutable (Marie Forleo)
* Question the Drink (Kari Schwear)

I go into depth about Profit Without Worry in Chapter 6 of this book, so I am going to skip that 3 Word Rebellion for now. Let's analyze the 3 Word Rebellions Everything is Figureoutable and Question the Drink.

*Everything is Figureoutable*, who hasn't needed that reminder when running a business, right? Marie Forleo created a movement and a highly successful business around these three words. But why? **It's useful to her right people**. It reassures them that they've got this!

Marie's business caters to the new business owner just starting out on this grand adventure. She knows that they'll experience amazing highs and devastating lows. During those lows, Marie's message whispers in their ears, "Everything is Figureoutable." It's the reminder that we give to our friends in the midst of a business struggle or even a life crisis. When we tell others about Marie's message, we are spreading her message, we are helping her grow her movement, and we are even giving people a place to belong during hard times.

*Question the Drink* straddles the line between a Battle Cry (because it starts with a verb) and a Declaration. To me, this 3 Word Rebellion serves as a Declaration because it reminds Kari's clients to always question that drink they are thinking of having.

Kari works in a relatively new area of coaching around alcohol called Gray Area Drinking. The people she works with don't have a problem with alcohol that rises to the level of Alcoholics Anonymous, and they also don't think they have the healthiest relationship with drinking. Kari grabs their attention by letting each person know that they can Question the Drink, which piques their curiosity and also lets people who don't know about her business have an important realization. While they work with Kari to improve their relationship with alcohol, they can use Question the Drink as their mantra. **The bottom line is: Question the Drink attracts new people to her business while providing an important touchstone for her existing clients.**

THE REBEL TRUTH:

# IT DOESN'T MATTER

IF YOU CHOOSE A BATTLE CRY OR NAMING THE CHANGE OR A DECLARATION AS YOUR 3 WORD REBELLION FORMAT.
**PLAY WITH THEM
AS YOU DO YOUR ANALYSIS!**

# CREATIVE CONSTRAINT #2:
# BE POSITIVE

In the last chapter, we discussed how it isn't enough to rebel; you must create a vision of the future for your audience. Paint a picture: Where are you leading them? What does it look like when you get there?

With this in mind, people want to be led to a brighter future. Your 3 Word Rebellion is the light that guides them there. So you want to avoid negative words like *don't, not, stop,* etc.

The one caveat I would place on this constraint (rules are made to be broken) is if the brighter future is already agreed upon by the people in your movement. For instance the students at the high school in Parkland, Florida, where 17 teachers and students were massacred, started the #NeverAgain movement to hold politicians' feet to the fire and change gun laws. The future they are painting is one where kids aren't gunned down in school. It's clear that "never again" means that there is never again a shooting in a school.

In most cases, your 3 Word Rebellion should be a positive statement. Avoid the word *not* because it keeps your rebellion rooted in what's wrong.

What do you do if you have negative words in your word bank? Easy fix. Simply go to thesaurus.com or WordHippo.com, type in the word, and look for the antonyms.

# CREATIVE CONSTRAINT #3: KEEP IT TO TWO TO FIVE WORDS

A three-word phrase tends to be the easiest for the audience to remember, repeat, and tell others. Three words easily turn into a hashtag. Three is a very magical number in writing, rhetoric, science, and religion. It is said that celebrity deaths happen in threes. In Christianity, there is the Father, the Son, and the Holy Ghost. And some of the most memorable advertising slogans of all time are just three words: "Just Do It." "Finger Lickin' Good." "Yes, we can!"

In writing, the Rule of Three is said to be more interesting, potent, and even humorous to the audience. This is because humans are pattern spotters. For us to notice a pattern in something, there must be at least three instances of it. When we see something happening in threes, we notice it and commit it to memory.

Three is magical for spreading your message, yet I do believe a range is possible. I've noticed many two-word rebellions like #MeToo, "Got Milk?," and #NeverAgain. There have also been very successful rebellions that are more than three words.

So while I chose three for a reason, I'd rather give you flexibility within this constraint than be dogmatic that it *must* be three words.

I know as long as you keep your 3 Word Rebellion to between two and five words, it should be memorable. A five-word rebellion means you'll need to get more creative with that hashtag, but I know you're up for it.

**A pro tip for finding the two- to five-word rebellion: start with longer sentences and then edit them down to the essence.**

You can see how I do this in a video included in the 3 Word Rebellion toolkit at **drmichellemazur. com/download**.

ADDITIONAL RESOURCE ALERT!

## CREATIVE CONSTRAINT #4: IT'S NOT ABOUT YOU

One of my mantras about speaking and communication is that it's never about *you*. All communication begins and ends with the people you serve with your message.

Similarly, your 3 Word Rebellion is not about you. It's about calling in your people, inciting them to act, and inspiring them to be the messengers of your message. If a 3 Word Rebellion is about you, it does not inspire people to be part of a movement.

What is the tell-tale sign that the 3 Word Rebellion is more about you than the audience? The use of self-referential pronouns.

Case in point, Hillary Clinton's 2016 campaign slogan, "I'm with Her." Living in Seattle, I saw so many yard signs with this slogan on it. Those signs told me one thing: their owners would be supporting Clinton. What they didn't tell me is what change Clinton stood for. This was a big mistake. A political campaign and a movement can never be about the leader of the movement. It has to be about what that leader stands for.

If you're tempted to use *I, her, him,* and so on...don't! This message that is bigger than your business needs to live and breathe beyond you. Make it about the change and the people your message serves.

# DON'T FORGET: GET A FRIEND!

One big warning before we dive in: do *not* attempt writing your 3 Word Rebellion on your own. Remember, this is the hard part. You're still too close to your message. When you try to analyze your work on your own, you'll discount what might be an awesome 3 Word Rebellion. You need help. (Check out the resources at the end of the book for how you can work with me on your 3 Word Rebellion.)

I highly recommend you ask one of your business besties to go through this process with you (better yet, buy them a copy of this book). Your 3 Word Rebellion comes from conversation with another person. It doesn't come from frustration and banging your head against the wall because you can't find it.

How do I know this?

My client Kathy showed up to our coaching session frustrated with herself. "Doc," she said (she loves to call me Doc), "I've been thinking about my 3 Word Rebellion for the past two weeks and I have no clue what it is."

I reassured her that it was extremely difficult to find your 3 Word Rebellion on your own and I was confident that we would find it together. Twenty minutes later, voilà! Her 3 Word Rebellion was in her free writing all along. She just needed someone else to show her the way.

Get a friend in the rebellion. Then apply these tips to make writing your 3 Word Rebellion fun!

# USE THIS SPACE OF INFINITE POSSIBILITY TO

## craft your own 3 word rebellion

_____

_____

_____

_____

_____

_____

_____

_____

_____

_____

_____

_____

_____

_____

_____

_____

_____

_____

_____

_____

_____

_____

_____

_____

_____

_____

_____

_____

_____

_____

_____

_____

_____

_____

_____

_____

_____

_____

_____

_____

_____

_____

_____

_____

_____

_____

_____

_____

_____

_____

_____

_____

# HOW YOU KNOW WHEN YOU'VE FOUND YOUR 3 WORD REBELLION

A frequently asked question about 3 Word Rebellions is, "How do I know if I've found the 'right' one?"

**First, I want to remind you that a 3 Word Rebellion is not forever.** There is no right or wrong. Your 3 Word Rebellion is not written on your tombstone... yet. It can (and will) evolve as you and your business evolve. You're not marrying it for eternity.

For years, I was describing my work with speakers as "Speak for Impact." I like that turn of phrase, but I didn't love it. While I very much love the word *impact*, it didn't feel expansive enough to me. It didn't feel rebellious enough. However, it was "good enough" to put out there and to name my profitable signature service after.

There is nothing wrong with "almost right." It's better to put your work out into the world with almost right, get feedback, and let it breathe so an evolution can take place, rather than hiding out until it's perfect.

**Second, get the idea of perfection out of your head.**

## PERFECTION IS A MYTH THAT STOPS YOU FROM TAKING ACTION.

If you get to "almost right" and can't find the "hell yes this is so right I can't believe it," go with it.

Remember, your 3 Word Rebellion can evolve. You might find your forever 3 Word Rebellion right now or you might not. Simon Sinek got known for Start with Why and has since moved on to Leaders Eat Last.

**Third, your 3 Word Rebellion should feel expansive yet a bit terrifying.** When you hit upon it, the common reaction is to feel unsure. Like, "Oh, this may be awesome, let me sit with it." That's normal. As you sit with it, you'll start seeing the possibilities of your rebellion grow before your eyes. When that happens you'll start feeling terrified. "Oh shit, why did this idea choose me?" is not an uncommon reaction.

**Finally, talk about it to other people (but not too many).** The goal of the 3 Word Rebellion is to create change, and you can't do that on your own. You need people. Start by telling the people you trust the most who will give you the best and most honest feedback. However, don't crowdsource it in your Facebook group or put it out to your email list. What is it they say about too many cooks?

As we wrap up this chapter, I want to encourage you to give this process time. Let it marinate and percolate. Get help. Talk to people. Hire a professional. Don't think it's going to happen in the blink of an eye (although for some people it does).

In the next chapter, I am going to give you some inspiration and analyze some 3 Word Rebellions in the wild so you can see what's possible for you.

# PROCLAIM YOUR 3 WORD REBELLION LOUD AND PROUD!

SNAP A PICTURE OF IT,
POST IT ON INSTAGRAM WITH
#3WORDREBELLION,
AND TAG ME @DRMICHELLEMAZUR.

# CHAPTER SIX:

# 3 Word Rebellion in the Wild

**R**ight now, I am sure there is one thing you need: INSPIRATION. I'm usually *not* a fan of inspiration because I think it's fleeting while action is priceless. But I do know that it helps to have role models of possibility when you're doing this work. This is one of the few times I'm delivering inspiration because I want it to incite action and the discovery of your 3 Word Rebellion.

Crafting your 3 Word Rebellion is daunting. You may be worrying, What if I don't nail it? What if I *do* nail it? What if I think I nailed it but then find out I didn't?

I get that this is a big deal. This is the message you'll be hanging your hat on for at least the foreseeable future. It's time to get out of your head and look for examples of 3 Word Rebellions to get your creative messaging juices flowing.

> IF YOU LOOK, YOU'LL SEE THAT 3 WORD REBELLIONS ARE ALL AROUND YOU, JUST LIKE LOVE.

When you start working on yours, you'll start seeing them *everywhere* (if you haven't already).

I find that when you can break down what makes other 3 Word Rebellions work, it becomes that much easier to find your own 3 Word Rebellion. Here are five case studies of 3 Word Rebellions that work. I explain why each one works and what makes them strong.

# CASE STUDY #1:
# POD SAVE AMERICA

Our first case study is one of my very, very favorite podcasts, *Pod Save America*. This podcast began right after the 2016 election when former Obama speechwriters and staffers Jon Favreau, Jon Lovett, Tommy Vietor, and Dan Pfeiffer decided to start their own media empire called Crooked Media.

They wanted to launch their flagship podcast that would anchor the whole media company. But a day or two before they were going to launch the podcast, they still didn't really have a name for it. Imagine being ready to launch a new product and not having a name for it. The pressure was on!

So they kept at it, and after rejecting some truly horrible names they eventually they came up with Pod Save America.

## WHY DOES POD SAVE AMERICA WORK AS A 3 WORD REBELLION?

First, it names the agent of change. If you are unsatisfied with politics right now, you know by the name that this podcast wants to make a change in the current political system. It's clear what you should be doing to take action—namely listening to their podcast.

This 3 Word Rebellion also works particularly well because they are playing with a tried and true phrase that we hear all the time. They simply switched out one letter of "God save America" and came up with Pod Save America. Because the name instantly reminds you of that famous phrase, Pod Save America is easy to remember.

If you're feeling stuck on your 3 Word Rebellion, ask yourself if there is a common turn of phrase that you could put your own unique twist on. If there is, it's a great way to find your 3 Word Rebellion.

## CASE STUDY #2:
## PROFIT WITHOUT WORRY

This is one of my favorite 3 Word Rebellions that I ever co-created. My friend and client, Michelle Evans, is a marketing expert, and when she first came to me, she had a podcast called *"The Marketing Funnel Show."*

On a scale of one to ten, with one being "I'd rather be cleaning my cat's litter box than listening to this podcast" to 10 being "So excited that I'll drop everything to tune in," how excited are you to tune in to The Marketing Funnel show?

I'm guessing you're more on the litter box side of the excitement spectrum. Because when you hear "marketing funnel" what do you typically think of? Bro marketers who talk about how to "grease the wheel" and force people to open their wallets using sleazy, manipulative tactics. Right?

This is NOT Michelle's way of creating funnels with clients. But leading with the term "marketing funnel," in her potential clients' eyes, was keeping her pigeonholed. When she changed the name of her show to *"Profit without Worry,"* **her podcast downloads quadrupled overnight. Why did that happen?**

# WHY DOES PROFIT
# WITHOUT WORRY WORK?

Profit Without Worry instantly intrigues Michelle's right people and that's why her podcast downloads skyrocketed. A hallmark of an excellent 3 Word Rebellion is that it makes people lean forward and say, "*Oh, what does that mean? What does it mean for me?*"

When we initially came up with this 3 Word Rebellion, we tested it on some of her potential clients and people responded to it right away. During sales conversations, they said, "*Yes, I want to Profit without Worry. That sounds so great. How do I make it happen in my business?*"

Her 3 Word Rebellion promises her right people a big change that they want (profit) while leaving behind a behavior they don't want (worry). In fact, you can experiment with this as a template. What is the big one-word result that you can promise people? What is the undesirable behavior they can leave behind?

In Michelle's case, we took a boring, solution-based message and transformed it into a revolutionary result that her people want. Now, think about how you can do that with your message.

## CASE STUDY #3:
## CHOOSE WONDER OVER WORRY

The third case study comes from the title of Amber Rae's book *Choose Wonder Over Worry*. When I first heard the title of this book, I thought, "Yes, please. I need more wonder in my life" because I am a chronic worry wart! My second thought was, "Whoa, that's a great 3 Word Rebellion."

## WHY DOES CHOOSE WONDER OVER WORRY WORK?

The first reason is because you instantly get it. You know exactly what Amber's rebelling against (worry) and you know the change she wants to create (cultivating more wonder in your life).

The second reason is her 3 Word Rebellion is active. That short title tells you exactly what to do when you find yourself worrying. So now when I find myself in a state of worry, which is more often than I'd like to admit, I know that I must choose wonder. I must get curious about my worries and ask questions of those worries. This is so powerful because it's helping me trigger a new behavior when I find myself in a distressing one.

The third reason is that this 3 Word Rebellion also makes me curious to know more and it makes me curious to go out and buy her book. I want to know *how* I can choose wonder over worry.

Finally, it is memorable because of the alliteration of the words *wonder* and *worry*. She could have gone with something like "choose curiosity over worry," but *curiosity* has too many syllables, it's a mouthful to say, and it loses the alliteration. Choose Wonder Over Worry has a great rhythm that makes it memorable.

Choose Wonder Over Worry is one of my favorite 3 Word Rebellions. It also provides a great "template" for writing a 3 Word Rebellion. When you're talking about a behavioral transformation, use the word *over* to describe the transformation of going from one state to another.

# CASE STUDY #4:
# FLATTEN THE CURVE

When I released the Kindle version of this book during the pandemic, I wrote this case study during the middle of Washington State's "Stay Home. Stay Healthy" order. This is a great example of a Battle Cry is Flatten the Curve. I'll admit that it was several days into the first case of COVID-19 being reported in the state of Washington before it hit me that Flatten the Curve was a 3 Word Rebellion.

In case you slept through the COVID-19 pandemic, Flatten the Curve is a phrase that scientists coined to apply to any pandemic to describe how individuals can keep the number of cases of an infectious disease down so that hospitals are not overwhelmed with patients. Taking steps to Flatten the Curve ensures that the medical system does not collapse during a pandemic.

## WHY DOES
## FLATTEN THE CURVE WORK?

Scientists are not normally known for their plain-spoken ways. Let me first commend these scientists for communicating such an important concept in a memorable way. The more you need people to act on your 3 Word Rebellion, the more memorable and curiosity-provoking it must be. Flatten the Curve achieves that.

Flatten the Curve is memorable because *flatten* and *curve* are contrast words--these words are the opposite of each other. When you combine words that we don't expect to see together, it makes your message memorable for your audience and easier to spread. You would not expect "flatten" and "curve" to appear in the same phrase. It immediately catches your attention and makes you wonder, "*What curve needs to be flattened? Why does it need flattening?*"

Finally, this 3 Word Rebellion does an excellent job of inciting action because once you find out what it is, you also know there are steps that you can take to do something to Flatten the Curve. Flatten the Curve became shorthand for staying at home, not taking unnecessary trips, washing your hands, and coughing into your elbow. Everyone had easy action steps to take to be a part of the solution.

# CASE STUDY #5:
# UNCAGE YOUR EPIC CREDENTIAL

This case study is for any business owner who is in a crowded industry. When competition is fierce and there are many people who do what you do (think life coach, copywriter, web designer, etc.), your message should set you apart from your competition. Your 3 Word Rebellion tells the story of your difference in just a few words.

Meet Caroline Mays. She writes bios, except what she creates is so much more than a bio. The word "bio" is underselling the value of her work. Her bios are epic, one-page stories that not only establish credibility but make an emotional connection with an audience.

When I met Caroline, she was frustrated that potential clients weren't getting the value of her work. She was unlike any other bio writer out there, but how did she get that across without using the word "bio?"

After she went through the freewriting process (the one you're doing in this book), we unearthed Uncage Your Epic Credential and finally found a way to communicate her work without using the dreaded B word.

## WHY DOES UNCAGE YOUR EPIC CREDENTIAL WORK?

Tell me, do you want a bio or an epic credential? For me, the answer is 100% the latter. Like the other 3 Word Rebellions, this one piques your curiosity about what an Epic Credential is. Then it makes you wonder what your epic credential could be. In this case, the message is building desire. It's promising an extraordinary result that will elevate your authority over all the other bios out there.

It sets Caroline apart from all the writers doing the same kind of work. There are thousands of writers who can write a solid bio for you, but there's only one person who can create an epic credential.

Finally, being the word nerd that I am, I love an unusual verb. Uncage is not a verb you hear in everyday conversation. It's a scroll stopper. The word itself implies an experience that is freeing and a bit wild. Uncage Your Epic Credential is an experience waiting to happen for your business, and that's why it works to bring clients to her door.

## SPOT 3 WORD REBELLIONS IN THE WILD

Now, I want you to put down your work on your own 3 Word Rebellion and take a little time to spot a 3 Word Rebellion in the wild. Once you find one, answer the following questions about it. When you know why other 3 Word Rebellions work, you'll have an easier time writing your own.

1. What is the 3 Word Rebellion you spotted in the wild?
2. What is it rebelling against?
3. What is the change it wants to create?
4. Is it a Battle Cry or Naming the Change or Declaration?
5. Any other observations on why it works?

Now that you've done your own analysis and you've been inspired by possibility, take a break. Grab a beer. Watch Netflix. Tomorrow, head back to Chapter Five and start reworking your own 3 Word Rebellion by brainstorming and applying the constraints.

Once you've found (or are even circling) your 3 Word Rebellion, your mind asks, *"will this work?"* Turn to the next page to see if your 3 Word Rebellion passes the test.

# CHAPTER SEVEN

# The Ultimate 3 Word Rebellion Test

ow do you *really* know if your 3 Word Rebellion will work?

For years now, I've had people slide into my Instagram direct messages (DMs) to ask me what I think about their 3 Word Rebellion. For the most part, I always answered that I didn't know.

Because without me understanding their industry or their ideal client and audience, I would be guessing if their 3 Word Rebellion is any good. When people work with me on this, I know ALL of those factors and can help guide them.

It became clear that I needed a way to help people assess their 3 Word Rebellions beyond asking your favorite clients and testing it out in your marketing. Although those ways work well, I find that people are hesitant to launch their rebellion until they know it's up to the task of capturing attention. This is ironic because the only way to be 100% sure is to put it out there and let people respond.

However, I wanted to solve my problem of people sliding in my DMs for expert advice and give them a simple test they could use to have an initial boost of confidence that their 3 Word Rebellion could work. That's why I created the Intrigue Loop as the ultimate test of a 3 Word Rebellion. In this chapter, we will talk about what the intrigue loop is and how to run your own 3 Word Rebellion through the loop to see if it passes the test.

## WHAT IS THE INTRIGUE LOOP?

Your 3 Word Rebellion has 3 jobs when it comes to your business. Job #1 is to **grab people's attention**. You want them to stop their scrolling; linger on your website a bit longer to find out more. Job #2 is to **make people think** about your work. Job #3 is to **grow your audience into a movement.**

Your 3 Word Rebellion must create intrigue to accomplish all three tasks. It must provoke curiosity and make people think. This is at the heart of the Intrigue Loop. The Intrigue Loop tells you if your message is a dead-end or if it actually has wings to capture the hearts and minds of your audience.

## HOW DOES
## THE INTRIGUE LOOP WORK?

Intrigue is the science of curiosity. When someone encounters your 3 Word Rebellion, you want them to ask two questions:

* What does it mean?
* What does it mean for me?

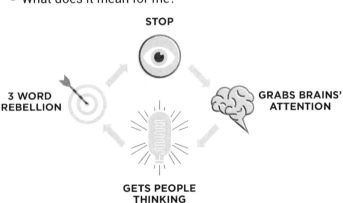

STOP

3 WORD REBELLION

GRABS BRAINS' ATTENTION

GETS PEOPLE THINKING

Let's take an example of a famous 3 Word Rebellion, *Start with Why*. When we encounter this message. It makes you think *"Oh, I should start with my why. Interesting, never thought about it before."*

Start with Why grabs the brain's attention. It tells us the starting place for our business (and our lives). Then immediately, your brain fires off the next question "What is my why? I don't know. I better figure it out if I am supposed to start there."

> THE MOMENT SOMEONE THINKS ABOUT A MESSAGE AND ASKS HOW IT APPLIES TO THEM THEY ARE HOOKED.

The question must be resolved. So, what do they do? They google "Start with Why." They find Simon Sinek's TED Talk. They watch it. They go to his website to learn more. They buy the book. Then take the course. They are now on a quest to satisfy their curiosity.

This absolutely happened to me when I heard Mel Robbins' 5-Second Rule. My brain said "What is that? Should I be following that rule?" Then I googled the 5-Second Rule to find out what it is. I bought her book, The *5-Second Planner*. Now, I'm Mel Robbins for life, pretty cool eh?

# WHAT DOES A DEAD-END MESSAGE LOOK LIKE?

At the end of 2020, I recorded an episode on the Rebel Uprising podcast about the 10 Messages that Need to Drown in the Sea of Sameness in 2021.

They included marketing messages like "Scale Your Business" or "Live Your Best Life" or "Find Your Voice." All of these look like 3 Word Rebellions, but they fail the Intrigue Loop test. Check this out.

You're on a life coach's website and you read "Live Your Best Life." Does that make you slow your scroll? Does it grab your attention? No, because it's what so many life coaches have on their website.

More importantly, **it doesn't make you think about YOU** or reflect on what it means for you. It's a dead-end message that makes people's valuable work get missed. Live Your Best Life is not a message that demands attention.

In the last chapter, I introduced you to my client, Michelle Evans. You may remember that before we worked together, her podcast was titled "The Marketing Funnel Show." It didn't have intrigue; it didn't make you want to go check out her show. In short, it was a dead-end message.

When we developed her 3 Word Rebellion, Profit Without Worry, and her podcast downloads exponentially increased, the message began to resonate. Why? **Her 3 Word Rebellion passed the Intrigue Loop test.**

Your mission with your 3 Word Rebellion is to do the same. You want to create a message that demands attention. A message that makes people scratch their heads and say, "*Oh, that's fascinating. Tell me more.*" Your 3 Word Rebellion makes people stop in their tracks.

## INTRIGUE LEADS TO ACTION!

**Now it's your turn!**

## WRITE YOUR 3 WORD REBELLION HERE:

_____

Now, ask yourself this:

## "WILL IT GRAB ATTENTION? WILL IT MAKE PEOPLE LEAN FORWARD AND WONDER WHAT IT MEANS?"

If no, stop right there. You're at a dead end. It's time to go back to chapter 5 and revisit your word bank to experiment and play some more.

If yes, go on to question #2.

## DOES IT MAKE PEOPLE THINK? DO THEY WONDER, "WHAT DOES THAT MESSAGE MEAN FOR ME?"

If you answered, no. Stop right there. You're at a dead end. Go back to chapter 5 and revisit your word bank.

## IF YOU SAID, "HECK, YES IT WILL!"— CONGRATULATIONS, YOU'VE PASSED THE INTRIGUE LOOP TEST!

Give yourself a high-five for doing all of this work. Now, it's time to put your 3 Word Rebellion out into the world.

Which is exactly what we are going to talk about in the next chapter of the book, launching your rebellion. Because creating your 3 Word Rebellion is just the start of the business and movement you're growing!

# Congratulations!

## FINDING YOUR 3 WORD REBELLION IS A HUGE ACHIEVEMENT.

DO SOMETHING TO CELEBRATE!

IN THE NEXT CHAPTER, I'LL SHOW YOU HOW TO GET YOUR 3 WORD REBELLION OUT INTO THE WORLD.

CHAPTER EIGHT:

# Support Your Rebellion

O nce you have your 3 Word Rebellion, the natural questions are, What's next? How do I launch it into the world? Are those three words enough to attract people to the movement I'm creating? Are they enough to incite action? Are they enough to get my message to spread?

While the 3 Word Rebellion is the hook that gets people interested and curious about what you're creating, you'll need something more to get people to raise their hand and say yes to what you're doing. **Once you've got their attention, what do you do with it?**

Ideally, you want people to join your movement. Sign up for your email community, hire you, or book you for podcast interviews or speaking engagements. What's the next step to capitalize on this attention and make those action happen?

**It begins with more messaging!**

Surprise! One of the first roadblocks I hit when I launched the 3 Word Rebellion is that I had no mother lovin' clue how to talk about it in a compelling way that would resonate with my right people (side note: you are my right people since you're reading this book; so, I figured it out).

I imagined Simon Sinek, when he first developed Start with Why, roaming the streets of downtown Seattle, repeating his message over and over with NO ONE RESPONDING.

That's what happens when you don't know how to talk about your business, your 3 Word Rebellion, or your movement—people don't respond or take action.

Luckily for Simon, he knew how to talk about Start with Why so that once he got your attention with his 3 Word Rebellion, he knew what to say to get you to take action to find your why.

There are two essential pieces of messaging that help your 3 Word Rebellion take flight: the Client Decision Journey and Signature Stories.

But before we can go there, we need to take a look at who you started this business and movement for in the first place—**your audience and your clients**. Because, to paraphrase Bryan Adams, "Everything you do...you do it for your peeps."

## HOW TO SUPPORT YOUR AUDIENCE TO JOIN YOUR MOVEMENT & SAY YES TO YOUR BUSINESS

Your 3 Word Rebellion is making a mighty big ask of your audience—and heck, your business or speaking is already making this ask—you're asking your audience to change. Sure, it's easy to think that this transformation will help people. You're 100% right. However, human beings are extremely resistant to changing the status quo.

We see proof of this on January 1st every single year. Throngs of people decide to create a New Year's resolution that they are going to stick to, and a few weeks later they have totally dropped it. That's because change is uncomfortable, while the status quo is quite cozy.

Your 3 World Rebellion is all about creating change. And creating change in a system, any system—on the personal level, the industry level, or even the societal level—causes a great deal of discomfort.

YOU MUST EASE THAT DISCOMFORT
SO THAT YOUR 3 WORD REBELLION
INCITES ACTION.

You want to help people break through that resistance and discomfort around change so they can enthusiastically join your movement. The first step in achieving this is getting to know them.

REBEL TRUTH:

# YOU CAN'T CREATE A MOVEMENT ON YOUR OWN. YOU NEED PEOPLE.

YOU CAN'T CREATE
A BUSINESS ON YOUR OWN.
YOU NEED PEOPLE.

YOU CAN'T CREATE
A SPEAKING BUSINESS
WITHOUT A PLATFORM.
YOU NEED PEOPLE.

# LEADERS LIKE YOU NEED PEOPLE TO FOLLOW YOU.

## KNOW YOUR AUDIENCE

You need people to enroll in the change that you're trying to create, and to do that you must understand the people you want to join you in your movement and your business. Once you know your audience, you can create Rebellious Talking Points that fuel your Client Decision Journey. These points are grounded in what they need to hear to join your movement.

Most importantly, these points must resonate with your right people to turn strangers into clients.

To get to know their audience, the first thing I do with my clients is ask them very standard questions about their audience demographics and psychographics.

## HOW IS THE SYSTEM KEEPING YOUR AUDIENCE DOWN?

We move on to the most critical questions, about how their audience feels challenged. What are their problems? How is the system keeping them down?

For the business owners and entrepreneurs I work with, they rely solely on word of mouth marketing because they don't know how to communicate the value of their work. Finding that message they want to be known for is hard. It's a huge struggle (as I am sure you now know). While you can run a successful business without a strong message, at some point you'll plateau because your message isn't attracting the right people. The lack of a message prevents you from growing bigger, but the 3 Word Rebellion helps with that.

Another example from my own work: With my clients who are speakers, the industry keeps them down by not paying them for their work. There are too many speakers out there doing it for free. There's too much supply and not enough demand, and event organizers want to make a profit on their business. That means speakers must stand out and create something unique and have their own platform that they can leverage so they can get paid, and the 3 Word Rebellion helps with that.

So that's the first set of critical questions. What are your audience's challenges? How has the system been keeping them down?

## WHAT DO THEY BELIEVE?

The second set of critical questions is around their beliefs about your 3 Word Rebellion—the good beliefs, the bad beliefs, and the ugly beliefs—because beliefs are the key thing keeping your audience from taking action on your message.

Now, most people, when they hear me talk about the 3 Word Rebellion, they're excited about it. They're curious. They want to know what their 3 Word Rebellion is.

Those are great beliefs that I can use when I'm talking about the 3 Word Rebellion! I do talk about that curiosity and excitement. At the same time, I know it terrifies people to think about creating a message bigger than their business, one that takes on a life of its own and that they don't have control over. It's a big ask.

So my job is to address all of those beliefs (positive and

negative), and we do this by using what's called Inoculation Theory. Allow me to geek out on this for just a moment with you. When you apply this theory, you'll get people moving toward yes.

Developed by social psychologist William McGuire in 1961, the Inoculation Theory posits that you should address the beliefs that the audience has about your argument, especially if they are negative beliefs. Talk to them about each negative belief and after you acknowledge it, make an argument to counter that belief so you can bust through their resistance and help them step closer to yes.

This theory does two things for you in your communication. Number one, it shows the audience that you deeply understand them and their challenges and their beliefs, and that creates goodwill and trust. Number two, it gives the audience a way forward. It shows them that their belief can be challenged and that it can be changed, so they're more willing to accept your message.

## CREATE YOUR
## REBELLIOUS TALKING POINTS

Now that you have a better understanding of your audience, you can create talking points to address their challenges and beliefs and encourage them to join you. Your Rebellious Talking Points become the core of your messaging. They are the support for your 3 Word Rebellion. They are the journey you take the audience (or customer) on so they will become the messengers of your message and your clients. These are the essential conversations that you need to have to incite action with your audience and have them join your movement. These talking points are what you talk about on podcasts, on the stage, during a webinar, on TV, on Instagram, in your artwork, and so on.

TO BRAINSTORM WHAT YOUR
TALKING POINTS SHOULD BE,

# *consider these questions:*

WHAT CHALLENGES NEED TO BE
ADDRESSED TO GET
THE AUDIENCE TO YES?

_____

_____

_____

_____

_____

_____

_____

_____

_____

_____

_____

_____

_____

_____

_____

_____

_____

_____

_____

# What beliefs

## NEED TO BE ADDRESSED?

_____

_____

_____

_____

_____

_____

_____

_____

_____

_____

_____

_____

_____

_____

_____

_____

_____

_____

_____

_____

_____

_____

# How do you define

## YOUR 3 WORD REBELLION?

Go deep here. Don't just write a one or two sentence answer.
Describe what it looks, feels, smells, sounds, and tastes like.

_____

_____

_____

_____

_____

_____

_____

_____

_____

_____

_____

_____

_____

_____

_____

_____

_____

_____

_____

_____

# WHAT DOES YOUR
# 3 WORD REBELLION
## want people to know?

_____

_____

_____

_____

_____

_____

_____

_____

_____

_____

_____

_____

_____

_____

_____

_____

_____

_____

## SUPPORT YOUR TALKING POINTS AND STRIKE AN EMOTIONAL CHORD

Once you have your Rebellious Talking Points, you need support for each of those talking points. Support can be your stories, your clients' stories, famous people's stories, case studies, and even research and statistics. Huzzah!

The point of this support is to not only show that your Rebellious Talking Points are in fact true, but to also strike an emotional chord with your audience. **Emotion drives action, always.**

One question that I ask my clients is, How do you want the audience to feel after each of your Rebellious Talking Points? Angry? Sad? Empowered? Inspired? Happy?

# What is the emotion
## THAT YOU WANT TO INSPIRE?

_____

_____

_____

_____

_____

_____

Now that you know, you can start brainstorming different stories that you can tell about your 3 Word Rebellion to further remove your audience's resistance and move them ever closer to saying yes to your rebellion.

Now, a big old caveat for storytelling. Telling your story is important for the audience to connect with you, but there's a mistake I see people make when they tell their story: they make themselves the hero of the story. When you make yourself the hero of the story, it actually disconnects the audience from you. The audience thinks, Wow, that's interesting—I sure hope it all works out for you—now let me find someone who includes me in what they want to build.

In his book *Building a StoryBrand*, Donald Miller argues that you should position yourself as the guide and never the hero of the story. You want to show the audience that you solve a problem for them. You want to be more Yoda than Luke, more Dumbledore than Harry Potter, more Haymitch than Katniss.

To do this, you want to employ a technique I call the story turnaround. Basically, you need to find the moral of the story that creates a teachable moment for the audience. Just like fairy tales often have a moral to the story that children can learn and grow from, you're giving your people the moral to the stories you tell and moving them to act on your 3 Word Rebellion.

Here's your next mission: Take some time to brainstorm the stories you want to tell. Don't try to make them fit under any one talking point (some stories could fit under every talking point); just answer the following questions to start:

# What stories about you
## CAN *YOU* TELL? WHAT IS THE STORY TURN AROUND FOR EACH ONE?

_____

_____

_____

_____

_____

_____

_____

_____

_____

_____

_____

_____

_____

_____

_____

_____

_____

# What client stories

## CAN YOU TELL?

_____

_____

_____

_____

_____

_____

_____

_____

_____

_____

_____

_____

_____

_____

_____

_____

_____

_____

_____

_____

_____

# What stories about

## FAMOUS OR FICTIONAL PEOPLE RELATE TO YOUR 3 WORD REBELLION?

_____
_____
_____
_____
_____
_____
_____
_____
_____
_____
_____
_____
_____
_____
_____
_____
_____
_____

# WHAT RESEARCH/
# CASE STUDIES/STATISTICS
# CAN YOU USE TO SUPPORT
# your 3 Word Rebellion?

_____

_____

_____

_____

_____

_____

_____

_____

_____

_____

_____

_____

_____

_____

_____

_____

_____

_____

_____

_____

Now that you've brainstormed the stories, go back and look at the Rebellious Talking Points you created and classify the stories around the points they most support. Don't worry about using a story more than once. Repetition is important here.

When you repeat your stories, your audience remembers your stories. The more they hear your stories, the more likely they will share your stories. The goal is to make your story a story your audience can tell.

Now that you have *all* the messages you need to launch your 3 Word Rebellion, it's time for the final part: crafting the audience journey to incite action.

# CRAFT YOUR CLIENT DECISION JOURNEY

The client decision journey is where all your hard work comes together to plot a course to move your audience to action. It's how you influence people to join the movement you're creating, act on the change you've identified, and tell others about your rebellion. This journey is how you ethically persuade people to become your client. **The client decision journey leads your audience to buying from you.**

The client decision journey starts with your people's biggest area of resistance or their most pressing challenge. Revisit the "Know Your Audience" section and choose the starting point. Remember to speak with empathy about the challenge they are facing. You want to get this journey started off on the right foot. Poking at pain points is the equivalent to repeatedly kicking someone in their broken leg whereas empathy starts with understanding and acknowledging their challenge.

The client decision journey ends with acceptance of your 3 Word Rebellion and your future client hiring you. On the way to that destination, you need to hit certain messaging marks to get that person to an unequivocal yes. **Messaging marks are decision points where the person interested in your message commits to acting.**

These marks include helping diagnose the real problem your audience member faces, establishing know, like, and trust, showing how you uniquely solve the problem they are facing, and ultimately getting them to raise their hand and say yes to your offer.

At each of these messaging marks, your audience member aka your future clients make decisions about whether to take the next step with you. They decide things like:

* Whether or not to connect or engage with you on social media
* Visit your website to check out your work
* Sign up for your email list because they have a problem you help them with
* Booking a consultation with you to find out about your services
* Buying your products and services

The talking points and the stories are the support needed to hit these messaging marks, remove resistance, and get your audience into action. You are making an argument for why they should say yes, why they should act, and why they should get involved with the change you are creating. You'll need to put yourself in your audience's shoes and think about the order of the talking points and which story or piece of support will be most compelling to them on their journey to yes.

Before you start creating your own Client Decision Journey, here's an example of my journey when someone *discovers me on a podcast.*

There are three topics I'm consistently interviewed for on podcasts (yes, all the angles come from my messaging):

* Standing out in a noisy space with dwindling attention spans
* Bro Marketing
* My business identity crisis

When they decide to tune in, they will **hear these key messages regardless of the podcast pitch angle.**

* Why marketing doesn't work aka why messaging is foundational to your business
* What's a 3 Word Rebellion and why it's important in business
* What makes certain 3 Word Rebellion so sticky and attention-grabbing
* A case study or two of my clients' 3 Word Rebellions and their results

At this point, **the listener can decide to ignore me because they don't have a messaging problem, or they decide to:**

* Buy the book
* Download the 3 Word Rebellion taster
* Follow me on Insta or LinkedIn

If they do that, they get more information that **helps them decide to work with me:**

* The 3WR process and framework
* How to know if you're ready for messaging
* The other pieces of messaging you need to market your business

* How to work with me
* Case studies that showcase different results

This leads to the final decision my potential client makes on this journey:

* Book a consult
* Don't book a consult

Your business and budding movement must have these essential pieces of messaging: the 3 Word Rebellion, Rebellious Talking Points, and Story to convert strangers into clients and the messengers of your message.

On the next page, fill out the Client Decision Journey Map and use it as the compass to build your business and your movement and guide your audience to action.

When you have this map in place, you will be unstoppable in sharing your message because you'll always know exactly what to say to move people closer to saying yes to your business and your transformational offers. (And if you want help mapping out your client decision journey, you know I'd love to work with you on it **along with your 3 Word Rebellion.** Book a call at **www.3wrcall.com** to discuss.)

With your 3 Word Rebellion and supporting messaging in place, it's time to launch this message, grow your business, and build your movement. The best news: You don't have to wait to be chosen for a stage to start sharing this message. You can start sharing *now*! Let's launch your rebellion in the next chapter.

**ADDITIONAL RESOURCE ALERT!**

# Client Decision Journey Map

## 3 WORD  REBELLION

 **TALKING POINT**

 **TALKING POINT**

 **TALKING POINT**

 STORY #1

 STORY #1

 STORY #1

 STORY #2

 STORY #2

 STORY #2

# CHAPTER NINE

# Launch Your Rebellion

**C**ongratulations! You're ready to launch your 3 Word Rebellion and your movement. You've created the messaging that you need to grow your audience and your business.

Your 3 Word Rebellion doesn't do anyone any good if it dies in your workbook! It's time to get this message out into the world.

Take a deep breath. In this chapter, you'll decide and commit to a launch plan. Let's dive in.

## LAUNCH YOUR 3 WORD REBELLION WITH AN INCITING INCIDENT

Every movement has an inciting incident that kicks it off. When Rosa Parks refused to move to the back of the bus, little did she know that she was inciting a movement. When the school shooting happened in Parkland, Florida, little did we know that it would be the genesis of the #NeverAgain movement. Trayvon Martin's murder incited three black activists to start the Black Lives Matter movement.

The kind of movement you're creating does not have to start with a tragic event that incites action. However, your inciting incident will require bold, courageous action. In "The Art of Revolution," Jonathan Fields argues that businesses can create their own inciting incident when they are launching their movement.

When Apple launched the iPhone, Steve Jobs gave a speech to usher in the new technology that has changed almost everyone's life. His speech was an inciting incident.

When Elon Musk launched his red Tesla into space with Starman piloting the car, he was inciting an incident around SpaceX. He garnered lots of attention and had even non-space geeks buzzing about the work he is doing.

You don't have to have a big launch event or launch a car into space to create an inciting incident. In fact, every time your business communicates, it can be an inciting incident.

What can your inciting incident be?

* A speech that recruits people to your movement
* A workshop where people act on your message
* A webinar that spreads your message online
* A podcast interview with an influencer
* A media interview on national TV
* An Instagram Story or Facebook Live
* A piece of art or an exhibition
* A book (like this one)
* A guest blog post

Your entire brand can even be an inciting incident (more on that in a moment!).

There are so many different inciting incidents; it's up to you to decide which one is your best path or which combination you want to try. Regardless of what you choose, make sure you enjoy spreading your message that way.

WHEN YOU LOOK AT THAT LIST OF
POTENTIAL INCITING INCIDENTS, IN
THE SPACE BELOW WRITE DOWN
THE ONES THAT YOU WOULD
# most ENJOY creating?

_____

_____

_____

_____

_____

_____

_____

_____

_____

_____

_____

_____

_____

_____

_____

_____

_____

_____

_____

# CHOOSE YOURSELF
# AND YOUR REBELLION

Here's what I don't want you to get hung up on: waiting for someone to choose you to launch your 3 Word Rebellion in the world.

It's easy to think, "When I get the speaking gig/the media interview/the podcast interview/the exhibition/the book deal, I will launch this rebellion." No. **I want you to launch your rebellion now.** As your message gains momentum, there will be plenty of people wanting you for their stage, podcast, and TV show.

I encourage you to create your own damn stage. Host the webinar. Put on a live event or retreat. Jump on Facebook Live and share your 3 Word Rebellion. Do an Instagram Story. Create a video.

All those options are available to you! You must choose yourself and this message. Build your own following of fanatics and the rest will come.

Do I have your agreement on this? Good.

What's one thing you can do to move your message into the world?

WRITE IT IN THE SPACE BELOW
AND CHOOSE A DEADLINE.
RIGHT NOW.
I WANT YOU TO COME UP WITH
ONE INCITING INCIDENT
## and commit to it.

_____

_____

_____

_____

_____

_____

_____

_____

_____

_____

_____

_____

_____

_____

_____

_____

_____

_____

_____

_____

Now that you're all excited and have committed to a plan for launching your rebellion, let's have a little chat about what might happen next. There is a possibility that when you hop on Instagram, do the webinar, go live on Facebook, or whatever, you might not get much of a response at first.

My friend, this is okay and it's perfectly normal. It doesn't mean that your 3 Word Rebellion sucks or that you suck. (P.S. You're awesome, message or no message.) It just means people aren't paying attention—*yet*.

About eight years ago, I was in Vancouver and my hubby and I went to a teeny tiny club to see this South African band called the Parlotones. This band played arenas in South Africa. In Canada, they were playing to a room of 25 people.

What I remember most from that show was the opening act—they rocked. They had a big sound and were giving their all to that microscopic crowd. The band was Imagine Dragons. Since then, they have had three number one singles and won nine American Music Awards, nine Billboard Music Awards, and one Grammy. They play arenas now instead of tiny nightclubs.

The point: we all start at zero. When you first launch this message, you'll be playing to a small nightclub audience who is more interested in their drinks than what you're laying down. They might not respond and that's okay. Keep sharing your message. Share it until you're sick of it and then share it some more. The more you share, the more momentum you will build. Sharing consistently and often is how you break through the noise.

# THE THREE MOST IMPORTANT TYPES OF INCITING INCIDENTS

These Rebellious Talking Points and signature stories can easily be transformed into a speech, a workshop, or a retreat. You should also share them all over social media. I want to walk you through the three most useful types of inciting incidents, how you can use them, and how to know which is right for you.

## 3 WORD REBELLION AS A SPEECH/WORKSHOP/RETREAT

People tend to fall into one of two camps. Camp number one is "Hell yes, I want to be speaking," while camp number two is "No way, speaking isn't for me."

Either camp is A-OK with me.

HOWEVER, THE REBEL TRUTH IS:

# IF YOUR 3 WORD REBELLION GAINS MOMENTUM, YOU *WILL* BE ASKED TO SPEAK, ON STAGE OR VIRTUALLY.

YOU NEED TO BE PREPARED FOR THAT POSSIBILITY.

If you're in the hell-no-never-ever camp, keep reading this section anyway. You never know when a hell no will turn into a hell yes, especially after you read this pep talk on why speaking may be in your future.

I think that speaking is one of the best ways to launch your rebellion. (In full transparency, I am biased; speaking has been my jam since the 10th grade.) Speaking or running a live event is how you can connect with your people face to face. That connection is powerful. It builds trust much more quickly than other types of inciting incidents. It's invigorating to see the impact your 3 Word Rebellion has in real life.

## GIVE SPEAKING A GO AND WATCH YOUR MOVEMENT GROW.

So how do you create that speech or workshop or even webinar? Your Rebellious Talking Points become the points of the body of your speech, and the stories you created support those points. You already have a good 80% of the raw material for your signature keynote speech. Now it's about putting it together, marketing it, and seeking out places to speak.

It may seem like I am glossing over all the how-tos of launching your inciting incident with speaking, and I am. If you're interested in more of the how-tos of speaking, I've written two books on the subject: *Speak Up for Your Business* (which is a how-to-guide for giving a speech that makes the audience act) and *Speak for Impact* (a strategy guide for building a speaking business). Grab those two books on Amazon and get all the juicy details on speaking.

# 3 WORD REBELLION
# ON SOCIAL MEDIA

When you have your 3 Word Rebellion, your talking points, and the stories that you want your audience to share, you don't have to wait to land a speaking gig, be asked on a podcast, or be selected to lead a workshop at a retreat. You can start sharing that message *now*.

Like right now. In this age of Facebook Live, Instagram Stories, and a variety of other platforms, you get to create your own damn stage.

That's right: You get to remove the gatekeepers and build your own stage and invite people to follow you. You can share your 3 Word Rebellion, your Rebellious Talking Points, and your stories every day. How exciting is that?

Now you might be thinking, Do I really have to do it every day... like really? Yes, you do. Sharing your message consistently is the way you get known for your message. It's how you find that audience to build your movement. It's how those people become your messengers. You do all that by showing up consistently over time.

Where should you be showing up? It depends on two things. First, where is your audience hanging out? Second, where do you like to hang out?

In my business, I work with a lot of business owners who want to add corporate speaking and training into their business mix, so the best place for them to hang out is LinkedIn because that's where corporate folks hang out.

In my own business, I initially hung out on Facebook, and I still do Facebook Lives once a week. However, I found my real love in Instagram and Instagram Stories. My clients are on Instagram, and I enjoy watching others' Stories. I love following my clients on Instagram to find out what they are up to. It's the perfect place to launch my own rebellion.

Remember, every time you speak, you can incite action that gets people to say heck yes to your 3 Word Rebellion and to join your movement.

The bottom line is this...

> PICK A PLATFORM.
> LOVE IT FIERCELY.
> CREATE YOUR OWN DAMN STAGE.
> SHOW UP DAILY.

## 3 WORD REBELLION AS A BRAND

Your 3 Word Rebellion can (and should) be used as the core message of your brand. It will be the three words that attract your people. The people who want to hear from you. The people who want to follow you. The people who want to buy from you.

Imei Hsu is a perfect example of a person who is using her

rebellion as the keystone of her brand. Imei is an extraordinary woman. She's an IRONMAN finisher. She competes in ultramarathons. She has over 300 food allergies.

You read that right, 300 food allergies. What the heck does she eat? (Hint: meat, most veggies, and most fruits...and a ton of bacon!) You also might wonder how she gets enough calories in to support all of her training and activities (that's a struggle).

When Imei was diagnosed with celiac disease, she knew that she had to change *everything* about her eating. Eating one wrong food would land her in the hospital at worst or send her running for the nearest bathroom for hours at best.

She started to realize that she couldn't go to some of her favorite restaurants anymore because there was nothing on the menu she could eat. She had to decline invitations to hang out with friends because if she ate any of the food she would get sick. I invited Imei to my wedding, and I had to tell her that there was going to be nothing on the menu she could eat. She chipperly replied, "No problem, I'll bring my own food."

Even though she would gladly bring her own food, her food allergy was isolating. Worse, she had to figure out on her own what she could and couldn't eat. Sure, her doctor sent her to a nutritionist, but it wasn't very helpful. There were no other resources out there for navigating how to deal with a food allergy. So, she experimented on herself through trial and error and too many trips to the bathroom and the hospital to count.

When Imei and I started to work together, she was on a mission to give sufferers of celiac disease and other autoimmune diseases guidance and a roadmap so they would know what to do after they received a diagnosis. She wanted to mentor them on how to eat, how to prep their kitchen so it's a safe place to cook, and even what skin care products they could use (yep...even putting the wrong thing on their skin can make some people sick).

Imei is rebelling against a medical industry that is inadequately prepared to help people with food allergies and a restaurant industry that can't accommodate food allergies.

She wants her people to know that they are not alone. That there's a way to navigate this new food reality, and she could show them the way. In our sessions she would say, "I want to make food fun again."

BAM! There it was, her 3 Word Rebellion: Make Food Fun Again.

It clearly describes her mission and perfectly encapsulates the change she wants to create for her clients and the audiences who watch her speak.

If you go to Imei's website, myallergyadvocate.com, you'll see her 3 Word Rebellion featured prominently. And she's writing a book called, you guessed it, Make Food Fun Again. This is what she speaks on and what she will be known for in the food industry.

That's the power of the 3 Word Rebellion.

Like Imei, you can build your brand around your 3 Word Rebellion, and your brand can become the inciting incident for your movement.

# IT'S TIME TO LAUNCH
# YOUR REBELLION

Once you've found your 3 Word Rebellion (or it found you), it can be far too easy to hide it away or wait for just the right time to launch it into the world. My advice is to get it out there as quickly as possible. Yes, tell your business besties, your board of directors, your most trusted people first. Then launch it into the world.

When you have your Rebellious Talking Points and your stories, you must share your 3 Word Rebellion as soon as possible. In *Big Magic*, Elizabeth Gilbert writes about an idea she had for a book. Try as she might to write that book, life kept getting in the way. The book languished. It never got done.

A few years later, she ran into her friend Ann Patchett, who had just finished her latest book. She told Gilbert all about it: The plot. The characters. The twists and turns. Gilbert realized that Patchett had written the book that she could never finish. It was as if the idea for the book had literally jumped from Gilbert to Patchett because she was ready to write the book.

Your 3 Word Rebellion *will* find a way into the world. You can either be its messenger and take action on it now, or it will choose someone else. If this is your message, choose it. Choose to share it. Your 3 Word Rebellion is a living, breathing entity and it's longing to be shared.

Start today.

Your people, your industry, and the world are waiting to be transformed by your 3 Word Rebellion.

FINAL THOUGHT:

# Rebels Make Shit Happen

**Y**ou've done the work. You had a big aha, that feeling that finally, this is what you want to be known for. This is the message you were born to spread. If you haven't had that moment yet, trust me, it will come.

Now you have a choice. You can feel overwhelmed, like this message is too big, too important for one person to handle, and choose to hide the message away. Or you can feel overwhelmed, like this message is too big, too important for just one person to handle, and you can choose to start talking about it.

I chose to talk about it. I shared it with my people, and that's when I truly knew this was something bigger than me and my business. I knew that my gut wasn't lying when it told me that this is my next thing.

I tell you this because I know that it's easy to hide out when you have a breakthrough idea like your 3 Word Rebellion. Give yourself a week to bask, marvel, and delight in this idea. Admire its enormity. Feel gratitude to it for choosing you. See it as being outside of yourself and excited to change the world.

After a week, it's time to make shit happen.

You can start by slowly testing the idea out with your inner circle. Then it's go time! Start creating and launching your inciting incident into the world as soon as possible.

Let me be clear: It doesn't need to be a TED talk or an appearance on *Oprah* to launch your rebellion. It can be a webinar, a series of Facebook Lives, and announcing it on your podcast.

Getting your 3 Word Rebellion out there as soon as possible will give you invaluable feedback. So many people gave me input after my first workshop on this idea and helped form this book and refine my thinking around the 3 Word Rebellion.

It's your turn to make shit happen. Because I believe communication changes the world. I believe your 3 Word Rebellion chose you. I believe you are the perfect messenger for this message. I believe that you've got this.

Now I want you to commit to me—right here, right now—that you will get your 3 Word Rebellion out into the world. Launch your rebellion with an inciting incident, and make the difference you were born to make.

I, _____,

DO SOLEMNLY SWEAR THAT I WILL
GET _____

OUT INTO THE WORLD.

## THIS MESSAGE CHOSE ME.
## I AM THE PERFECT MESSENGER
## FOR IT.

I WILL LAUNCH MY 3 WORD
REBELLION BY DOING

_____

(YOUR INCITING INCIDENT)

BY _____.

(DATE)

I AM STOKED TO GET THIS
MESSAGE INTO THE WORLD!

THIS IS MY REBEL WORD,

_____

(YOUR SIGNATURE)

# Onward, Rebel! Onward.

# MOST AWESOME RESOURCES FOR LAUNCHING YOUR 3 WORD REBELLION

Best TEDx talk for finding your purpose:
"How Great Leaders Inspire Action" by Simon Sinek

Best kick in the ass to start taking action on your rebellion:
*The 5 Second Rule* by Mel Robbins

Want to know how to stand out from the crowd?
Check out *How the World Sees You* by Sally Hogshead

Need creative inspiration?
Read *Big Magic* by Elizabeth Gilbert

Best podcast for liberal-leaning politics junkies like me:
*Pod Save America*

Best resource for navigating the world of food allergies:
Look no further than Imei Hsu at myallergyadvocate.com

Ready to explore your relationship with alcohol?
Kari Schwear is the go-to with
Question the Drink at graytonic.com

Want your own epic credential?

Check out Caroline Mays at switchbladelemonade.com

## WANT THE BEST DAMN MESSAGING COACH IN THE WORLD?

*That's me.*

## TO WORK WITH ME ONE-ON-ONE, GO TO DRMICHELLEMAZUR.COM/3WR

# ACKNOWLEDGMENTS

This book would not have been possible without the support of my amazing, loving, and laid-back husband, Glenn Spaulding. Thank you, baby, for supporting the 3 Word Rebellion when it was just a bananas idea in my head. I cannot even begin to tell you what your support means as I've been building Communication Rebel over the years. You are my world.

To the amazing book coach Jennie Nash, one lunch with you changed my business and my life. Thank you for listening to me, seeing the patterns in what I was saying, and pointing it out. From the moment you said, "What about the 3 Word Speech?" I knew I was on to something. You rock.

To my incredible beta readers, David Fisher, Helen Thremetick, and Michelle Evans. How did I get so lucky to pick three people who would give me three entirely different perspectives of this book? Each of you made this book ten times better. Thank you for taking the time to read it and give your honest feedback.

Thank you to the two people who helped me get this book out into the world, Amy Scott and Natalie McGuire. Amy, you are a copyediting wizard. The book improved exponentially after being in your hands. Natalie, the only thing I can think to say to you is BOOBS! Seriously, you took my idea to make this book so beautiful that everyone would want to buy it into a reality. You're a creative genius who is a pure pleasure to work with.

To my mentors, Tanya Geisler, Tara McMullin, and Erika Lyremark, your guidance makes my vision possible. Tanya, thank you for holding a big vision for me. Tara, you're a strategic genius and my business grows whenever I follow your guidance. Erika, thank you for seeing the possibility in this work and helping me create a kick-ass service so that I could help others launch a million rebellions.

To my ladies, Rachel Alexandria, Tracey Warren, Rebecca West, and Maggie Patterson. Thank you for being the sounding board for my vision, giving me the support and accountability to rise up every day to achieve this vision.

To all of my clients, thank you for the trust you put in me. Thank you for sharing your stories and your message with me. The 3 Word Rebellion got better because of each of you.

To "the kittens" Samson, Brodie, and Attie, thank you for the purrs and cuddles. And THANK YOU for not deleting this book when you plopped on top of my laptop. More treats for you!

To my launch team, you all kick ass and I so appreciate your support in getting this book out into the world.

# ABOUT THE AUTHOR

Michelle Mazur, Ph.D. founded Communication Rebel® on the belief that communication changes the world, so that's what she helps business owners, entrepreneurs, and speakers do: rebel against the status quo to make a difference, one compelling message at a time. She is the creator of the 3 Word Rebellion™ for creating a message that matters to your audience so that you can build your business and your movement.

She is the host of the podcast *Rebel Uprising*, a podcast for the next generation of leaders who want to shake up the status quo and reach more people with their message. Dr. Michelle is the author of *Speak Up for Your Business* and the bestselling *Speak for Impact*. Her rebel yell has appeared in *Fast Company, Inc., Entrepreneur, PR Daily, Business2Community*, and *She Owns It*.

With over 25 years of experience and a Ph.D. in communication, Michelle has helped hundreds of business owners clarify their message, start their movements, and add thousands of dollars of revenue to their bottom line. The speakers she's worked with, some of whom have gone on to book $10,000 speaking gigs, become international speakers (even speaking in front of world leaders!), and raise three times the amount of money expected for the launch of a charity.

She lives in Seattle, Washington, with her adoring husband, three obsessive felines, and a huge collection of Duran Duran memorabilia.

Instagram is the best place to connect with Michelle (@drmichellemazur). Visit her website at **drmichellemazur.com.**

# ABOUT
# COMMUNICATION REBEL

**Communication Rebel exists to turn business owners, entrepreneurs, and speakers on the rise into the next generation of leaders and influencers. These Rebel Risers create a movement with their message by changing their audiences with their ideas while getting paid along the way.** We believe that communication has the power to change the world when the message matters and incites action.

In three months or less, we help business owners, coaches, and consults powerfully communicate the value their business creates, whether they are speaking to one person or a million people.

Our mission is to help experts and mutlpassionates who are excellent at what they do become known, sought-after, and even famous for their work.  is to become the premier message strategy agency for emerging thought leaders and influencers in the United States.

**Let's create a message that that grows your business and starts your movement!**

One of the toughest (and most important) things you'll do in your business is figure out your message. Your message is at the core of everything you do. Without a message, every time you sit down to write a blog post, pitch yourself for a podcast, or even write copy for a Facebook ad, it feels like a monumental task. You question yourself at every step and hope and pray that it works.

It's time to call in your audience, incite people to act, and inspire others to be the messengers of your message. It's your turn to be the thought leader and influencer on the stage, on podcasts, or in the media.

## MOST OF ALL, IT'S TIME TO QUIT STRUGGLING WITH WHAT TO SAY AND START MAKING A DIFFERENCE.

If you're done working and reworking your message
and want to shake up your industry,
you and Michelle could make a great team.

WE INVITE YOU TO CHECK OUT HOW
TO COLLABORATE WITH HER AT
DRMICHELLEMAZUR.COM/3WR

Printed in Great Britain
by Amazon